KAWASAKI—
SUNRISE TO Z1

OSPREY
COLLECTOR'S
LIBRARY

KAWASAKI—SUNRISE TO Z1

All singles, twins and triples plus the 900 fours—1962 to 1976

Roy Bacon

Published in 1984 by Osprey Publishing Limited
12–14 Long Acre, London WC2E 9LP
Member company of the George Philip Group

British Library Cataloguing in Publication Data

Bacon, Roy H.
Kawasaki—Sunrise to Z1.—(Osprey collector's library series)
1. Kawasaki motorcycle
I. Title
629.2'275 TL448
ISBN 0-85045-544-8

Editor Tim Parker
Design Gwyn Lewis
Filmset and printed in England by
BAS Printers Limited, Over Wallop, Hampshire

Contents

Mick Grant and Michio Uchida looking very pleased with the TT trophy won by Mick on a Kawasaki. Uchida was then managing director of the UK company

Foreword by Mick Grant

'Kawasaki lets the good times roll'—a one time promotional slogan—and good times they were. . . .

My association with Kawasaki motorcycles began in 1974, and went on for four years until the end of 1978. Mostly I road raced them, but as part of the deal I also aided their road bike marketing. This book, aptly called *KAWASAKI—SUNRISE TO Z1* is a superbly researched and fascinatingly catalogued account of Kawasaki's motorcycle history, well written by Roy Bacon, and is a must for Kawasaki enthusiasts wherever their particular interests lie.

After all these years of riding fast motorcycles I still find it hard to grasp that the Japanese have been involved in manufacturing motorcycles for so long that already many of their models are collector's items, being restored to original state and then shown at 'classic bike' shows. Unlike most British manufacturers for whom machines remained without major changes for, in some cases, decades and who produced small model ranges anyway, the Japanese from the start rushed in with many choices of machine and then threw modifications at them fast and furiously. So much so that without this type of book no record would exist of this most important and interesting era of motorcycle history.

Although small by Japanese standards, Kawasaki's motorcycle division—much more than any other Oriental manufacturer—has what could almost be described as a cult following. For who else are such affectionate nicknames such as 'Green Meanie', 'Team Green' or 'Kwaker' used whether the actual words are spoken in the UK, North America, Australia, France and even Japan? Their image was and is as one.

Reading through this book brought the memories flooding back. I recall, in particular, arriving in Hong Kong for the Macau Grand Prix in late 1977, and being wined and dined handsomely by the managing director of the ship building side of Kawasaki Heavy Industries. He took a party of us to Hong Kong's most famous hilltop restaurant for a traditional Chinese meal. A glorious affair until, with a solemn look, he passed me the head of a chicken with his chop sticks. I had read in horror of travellers in the Middle East having to eat sheep's eyes and the like, but I never expected it there. He must have (thankfully) seen the wild terror in my eyes and quickly burst out into hilarious laughter.

I, too, laughed with relief, but I must admit that I didn't see the funny side until some time later. The mention of Kawasaki will always conjure up many thoughts—some frustrating memories, but substantially happy ones.

You should enjoy this unique book.

Mick Grant
TT winner—1975 Senior, 1977 and 1978
Classics—with Kawasaki
Lepton, near Huddersfield, December 1983

Acknowledgements

I must admit to a real liking for Kawasaki motorcycles for I find them comfortable and easy to ride. Nearly all seem to fit me well which is half the battle and the staff at Slough (UK Kawasaki Motors headquarters) always make it a pleasure to call in to collect a machine or have a chat.

This book represented a step into the unknown Orient so before it was started, many discussions took place, and Tim Parker (my editor) and I thought hard and long before getting underway. We decided it was a go but might be difficult to write. Fortunately the task was made easy by the kind people at Kawasaki Motors UK and early discussions were held with the ever helpful Nick Jeffrey and Tony Jakeman. Equally forthcoming with advice and assistance was Peter Richardson of the Kawasaki Information Service who provides the company with a press and public relations facility in Great Britain.

Most of all I have to thank Dave Hill for all his patient help and for finding me material and pictures on many of the older models. His mine of information is very deep and very, very extensive so I asked him if he would check the manuscript. He did and the resulting corrections added to the story. His assistance made my job so much easier to do and he clarified many points for me.

The pictures came from a variety of sources. The early loco and aircraft were tracked down by the Osprey office; via the Science Museum in Kensington and an earlier publication of theirs in the Aircam series, respectively.

Many of the pictures came from Kawasaki material in one form or another and most of the others from the files of the magazines. Thus I am again indebted to Peter Law of *Motor Cycle News*, Jim Lindsay of *Mechanics*, Cyril Ayton of *Motorcycle Sport* and from the USA, editor Allan Girdler of *Cycle World* and librarians Otis Meyer and Jim Browker who helped Tim Parker in the CBS archive. One picture is from the old BSA press office at Small Heath, one from the Shell Photographic Service and one from *Trials and Motocross News*.

Among the Kawasaki supplied photos were some from Intercity Photography, part of the information service, and others from Murray Evans Associates who looked after the UK firm's press affairs in the mid-1970s. Pictures from the professionals included the work of Cecil Bailey, Russell Baty, Malcolm Carling, Stephen Colvin, Vaclav Hamsik, Jan Heese, Tim Parker and Coen Verburg. I even took a couple myself.

As usual all the pictures were returned to their files after publication and I have tried to make contact to clear copyright. If my letter failed to reach you or I have used an unmarked print without realising this, please accept my apologies.

To finish I must thank that super person and rider Mick Grant for kindly writing the foreword so quickly and easily and, as always, Tim Parker for putting up with me.

Roy Bacon
Niton, Isle of Wight
January 1984

1 Trains and boats and planes and—motorcycles?

Above **Very early Kawasaki steam locomotive from Edwardian times**

Top **Captured Kawasaki Ki.61-16 dating from WW2 with German style, in-line engine**

Kawasaki is unlike its major Oriental rivals for they are primarily if not originally motorcycle makers who happen to produce other items as well. Kawasaki Heavy Industries on the other hand is one of the world's largest industrial complexes and has interests in many fields on land, sea and in the air.

They happen to also build motorcycles but almost as a sideline and certainly at first for very different reasons to their competitors. This background has resulted in machines with their own flair and style with a tradition of excitement and speed. Away from their home country especially, the name Kawasaki has stood for performance on the street.

The origins of the firm go back to 1878 when Shozo Kawasaki founded a shipyard at Tsukiji, Tokyo, and steamships from there helped Japan's early colonising expeditions to Okinawa and Taiwan. In 1881 the Kawasaki Hyogo Shipyard was formed at Higashide-cho, Hyogo, and five years later the two yards were combined as Kawasaki Shipyard. A decade later, in 1896, this became incorporated with Kojiro Matsukata as president, and it began to gather momentum as a major company.

As early as 1901 Kawasaki developed Japan's first steam locomotive and in 1907 the Hyogo Branch Works were established to build locomotives, coaches, freight cars and bridge trusses, which gave them a toe-hold in structural civil engineering.

Four years later, in 1911, Kawasaki entered the field of marine transportation and began to lay the foundations of what was to become the K-line in 1919, this simple abbreviation a little easier for Western tongues than the full *Kawasaki Kisen Kaisha*. A year earlier, as Europe staggered to the end of a four year war, two more branches of the tree appeared, the first the Fukiai Works to produce sheet steel, which by then was a major need for both the shipping and railway sections. The second new branch took them into new areas and was the automobile and aircraft department and this brought them into the world of internal combustion engines and into the air.

Thus the Kawasaki empire rolled forward on land, sea and air as one of the original *zaibatsu*, the economic cartels that carried Japan from feudalism to a major industrial nation in so few years. In 1928 the Hyogo Branch Works became Kawasaki Rolling Stock and in 1937 the Fukiai Works became Kawasaki Aircraft with nearly two decades of aviation experience behind it.

The war years showed just how good Kawasaki aircraft engineering had become for they avoided the typical air-cooled radial engine with its massive frontal area to inhibit performance. Instead they build an in-line liquid cooled motor to power an army fighter called the Hien, and the Allies thought this to be of German origin so good was its performance.

The aircraft were built in a factory set up at Akashi in 1940 to produce both aero engines and fuselages, so this aspect of the business was transferred from Kobe. That site continued to be used for the ship building side.

After the war all but one sector of Kawasaki were fully employed in reconstruction and part of that job was to improve a totally inadequate transport system. The one part of the company standing idle was the aircraft division, so the engineering and manufacturing skills therein were turned to producing gears and gearboxes for the many small motorcycle firms that were mushrooming into life. In those early postwar years the choice for the citizen was to queue for a bus or tram which would be late, crammed full, slow and going in the wrong direction, or to walk.

Anything that could pull itself along under its own power was an improvement so almost overnight, first scores, and finally a hundred or more companies were building small machines and in need of supplies. Most performed badly and were poorly made, so producing better quality than the next factory was very easy for the Kawasaki team used to working to aircraft standards.

The Japanese motorcycle industry goes back to 1908 when a few pioneers began to experiment and build machines. The numbers built were miniscule for there were few roads in those days when most people travelled by boat. After World War 1 industrial expansion in Japan created a middle class that could afford their own transport and had the inclination to be

Modern Kawasaki electric locomotive used for passenger and freight hauling. One of many types built by the company

involved with such modern ideas. As motorcycles were cheaper than cars they began to be popular and their sale was advanced by the narrow roads of the times, really alleys and paths of a size that brought in a law restricting cars to 39 in. width. At that size they could at least cross the narrow bridges but it made for cramped accommodation.

At first foreign machines from England, Europe and the USA were popular and the flood of imports nearly killed off the Japanese industry. Then in 1922 the government brought in the Military Vehicle Subsidy Law that allowed them to give aid to makers or owners of machines suitable for military use as long as they were made in Japan. This immediately interested a number of major firms who decided to move into motorcycles.

At the head of the list and first off the mark was the Murato Iron Works with a copy of a Harley-Davidson, then one of the most popular of the imports and the basis of the Imperial Army's two-wheeled fleet. The two copies that the young founders of the company, Takaji Suzuki and Nobuji Murato, sent in were returned without comment and this was the fate of others. So they had a think about what was wrong and decided on a fresh but more modest approach.

Instead of trying to learn about the technology of the whole machine they decided to concentrate on one aspect, master that and move on to complete machines when they felt more ready. They chose the transmission as their field to become experts in, and in 1928 founded Meguro Seisakusho to build and supply gearboxes to the trade. This they did with success and the company prospered but at a time when the Western world was about to suffer a major economic crash followed by years of recession.

This was mirrored in Japan due to a major problem with balance of payments brought about by excessive imports, so the government became desperate to restrict these and increase home manufacture. At the same time military expansion dictated a need for motorized transport, and so during the 1930s tariffs were erected ever higher and the incentives to make all Japanese products increased.

At the start of the decade they benefited from a deal with Harley-Davidson. The American company needed cash and were happy to sell the drawings and tooling of an obsolete model which became the Rikuo and was quickly adapted for military use. The really useful part of the deal was not the machine details but the vital heat-treatment data for the steels, material specifications and a visit by senior production men. They showed how to set up a modern mass production factory, taught precision, interchangeable parts, clean workshop rules, assembly lines and the tricks needed to build complex and sophisticated machinery in quantity and to high quality standards.

In fact it is an essential facet of mass production that parts are made accurately and to these quality standards. If they are not they may not fit on assembly and so cause a bottleneck in production. If inaccurate or of too poor a quality to be used they have to be thrown away and because they have been made in quantity the useless parts stack up and need railway wagons to remove them. Thanks to the input of all this know-how, the bulk of the Japanese industry was jolted forward into modern times.

At Meguro they decided it was time to have another try at building a complete machine but by the mid-1930s found they were too late for the side-valve, big vee twin market which was taken up by copy Harleys. So they looked at European machines and settled on the 1935 Velocette MSS as a suitable one to copy. At that stage copying was by far the safest and quickest way of achieving something that worked acceptably well.

The result in 1937 was the Z97 with a twin port, single cylinder ohv engine of 500 cc that went into a rigid frame equipped with girder forks, and saddle for rider comfort. It pushed out 13 bhp at 3800 rpm and this gave a top speed of 60 mph which was a good deal less than the English original could achieve. For all that it was a good attempt and the result looked much as any English single of those times.

The Japanese industry was still in its infancy and production small with just over 3000 machines being built in 1940, the peak prewar year, and most of them were the Rikuo copy of the Harley and destined for the army. Another 18,000 Rikuo models followed in the period up to 1945.

It was not until 1948 that Meguro were able to restart production of motorcycles and with the Z97 came 250 and 350 cc ohv singles and a utility 125. Like all Meguros, the postwar range were well made and built to last, so establishing a reputation for reliability, ruggedness and long life. They were heavy machines with engines that turned over slowly but, in being so, could be relied on to last.

In 1954 they introduced the Z500 with single port 500 cc ohv engine, sprung frame and telescopic forks but without losing their traditional toughness.

About the same time they built their first twin called the Senior and this reflected comtemporary English design to a marked extent, except that the rear chain was fully enclosed. Handlebars tended to the high-rise style and the seat was two-level, but otherwise it was a typical ohv twin with primary chaincase on the left, telescopic and pivoted forks and full width front hub. They all sold well enough to make Meguro number two in Japan for a while, only behind Honda who made lightweights alone. Many of the Meguros went to the police.

LPG carrier built in one of Kawasaki's two huge shipyards situated at Kobe and Sakaide. Also one of many, including submersibles

They became involved with the historic Asama races held in the fifties to force on the development of home machines, and to that end the entire machine down to the last nut and bolt had to be made in Japan. No Dunlop, Bosch, Dell'Orto or Lucas parts to help out. 1957 was the best year for Meguro when they took the first two places in the 500 cc event plus 4th and 5th, with a Hosk in the third slot.

The winning machines had overhead camshaft single cylinder engines that pushed out around 30 bhp, nothing to worry a Manx Norton but more than sufficient to deal with the Japanese opposition.

Despite the brief exercise in modern thought the range remained essentially old fashioned,

although in 1959 the twin became the K1. This was a copy of the BSA A7 in general and its timing case and gearbox shell in particular, and an influencing factor must have been the success of the A10 at Asama that year, when imports were allowed to run. However, the case line was not altogether new as the 250 cc single had used it back in 1952.

It was a time of tremendous development in Japanese motorcycle engineering which was carried out behind an increasingly stiff tariff wall and then foreign currency control. Government agencies adopted a 'buy Japanese' policy and after 1955 the private citizen had no option but to buy the home product.

The one exception was to domestic manufacturers who paid no import duty to bring in a foreign machine they wanted to study. So they did just that and copied the best, just as others had done before them. The result was that by the end of the decade they were no longer copying but were building improved machines based on the very best German and Italian engineering.

In addition a vast docile home market allowed them to exploit the knowledge that sprang from the seed planted by the Harley engineers in 1930. They built modern factories, installed the very latest machine tools and by the late 1950s were the largest producer of motorcycles in the world, even though most of the world had never heard of them. There had been many casualties along the way and the decade had seen bitter competition, relentless price cutting and resourceful engineering driving out the weak and reinforcing the strong.

The hundred plus companies rapidly shrank to 50, then to 20, 15, 10 and to eight. In a few more years they were down to the big four, Honda, Suzuki, Yamaha—and Kawasaki. During this period Meguro lost out in sales for they dealt with a small speciality market, and then in 1960 they were hit by a strike and in stepped Kawasaki.

As soon as was possible after the war, the bulk of the Kawasaki empire was hard at work turning out its products as before, except the aircraft division which found itself with stockpiles of material and plenty of precision engineering knowledge but no customers for its normal output. So they turned their resources to meeting general transport needs and, like Meguro before them, began to make gears and transmissions for the many small motorcycle factories around them.

In 1949 they turned their attention to complete engine units and began the development and production of these. The first was the KE, an overhead valve single of 148 cc used by Fuji, Gasuden and IMC among others. It was followed in 1952 by the KH, a 250 cc four-stroke and the next year they established Meihatsu Industries as a subsidiary to build and sell complete machines. At the same time the KB-1, a 60 cc two-stroke engine unit was designed for use with bicycles. 1954 saw the Meihatsu 125 being built using the Kawasaki KB-5 engine and a scooter fitted with the KB-2 60 cc unit. This was developed from the KB-1 and the complete scooter carried the Kawasaki logo according to factory sources which, if true, make it the first Kawasaki two-wheeler. It is not mentioned in other sources and was most likely in limited production.

Left **Helicopters as well—and finally some motorcycles.**

Bottom **The 125 cc Meihatsu fitted with a Kawasaki engine**

Centre **Well built Meguro S8, a 250 cc ohv single that helped establish their rugged reputation**

Below **Meguro K1 500 cc twin modelled on a BSA and built from 1959**

Photographs of early Kawasakis are hard to find. These are taken from a factory publication

Bottom **The Kawasaki Pet M5 introduced in 1961. Typical 50 cc, three-speed, step-through**

Centre **First complete motorcycle built by Kawasaki, the 125 cc B7 sold as a Meihatsu in 1961**

Below **The Kobe assembly plant, B7s on line**

The 125 had an engine line not unlike that of the BSA Bantam and Yamaha YA-1, both descendants of the prewar German DKW. It was a straightforward unit construction job with a three port engine but did sport a central sparking plug. The kickstart lever went on the right and the gearchange on the left, while the engine was fed by a small carburettor fitted to the rear of the barrel. The engine unit went into a full loop frame with plunger suspension at the rear and telescopics at the front. The headlight fitted into a nacelle blended to the fork top and German influence was evident in the cantilever sprung saddle and small rear carrier mounted in lieu of a pillion seat.

By 1960 this design had become further influenced and changed by European work and the engine was now hung from a spine frame built up from pressings. The rear fork was made in the same way from pressings and at the front went a hefty pair of fork legs with short leading links at their base. Mudguards were sprung and massive with deep valances but still only one seat was provided. This was a pad just attached to the frame and behind it went a carrier with front rail. The centre section of the frame enclosed the ancillaries with toolbox covers on the sides.

Unfortunately they were never very good machines, being expensive and none too reliable so their sales only managed to just creep over 10,000 in their best year, 1959, before slipping back. In the same period the other companies were leaping forward technically and with sales so it was time for Kawasaki to review their two wheel policy.

Motorcycles had only been a temporary, minor offshoot to keep the aircraft division at work in the early postwar years. They had enjoyed very limited support at boardroom level and had little pressure to drive them forward in the manner of their competitors during that desperate decade. So it would have been an easy decision to stop building the tired Meihatsu line and to put the factory to other work.

The factor that stopped this happening was company image and the Kawasaki lack of it. At that time it was an industrial giant, well known and well respected in the fields of planes, ships, railways and construction but outside them unrecognized by the general public. Mention Kawasaki in Japan in those days and you either received a blank look or directions to the city between Tokyo and Yokohama. All rather irksome to a company of that size.

So they decided to move into a field where there would be public awareness, and with a motorcycle business already to hand the decision really made itself.

The results of this action began in 1959 with the establishment of a motorcycle production research department. From this work came a new assembly plant in Akashi completed in 1960 and late the same year Meguro became affiliated to Kawasaki Aircraft. While they had a limited range of machines, all rather dated, it was an improvement and a useful addition to those sold under the Meihatsu label. In addition they brought considerable motorcycle trading experience to the new, fledgling company and together they had a range that ran from 50 to 500 cc.

This link was reinforced in 1961 when there was a further corporate re-arrangement with Kawasaki Meihatsu becoming Kawasaki Jidosha Hantai with its headquarters built in Tokyo. On the machine side the first motorcycle completely built by Kawasaki was introduced as the B7 and initially sold under the Meihatsu label. It was a 125 cc two-stroke single coupled to a four-speed gearbox and owed nearly everything to the earlier Meihatsu, aside from the tank styling.

At the same time the M5 was launched, this being a step-through model with 50 cc single cylinder, two-stroke engine with three-speed

Left **Engine unit of 170 cc Meguro Ranger with unit construction and then rather dated style**

Below **The Kawasaki 250 cc SG built from 1964 to 1969 but firmly based on the older Meguro model**

gearbox. Construction followed the norm for such machines with low set spine frame that extended back to form a deep guard over the rear wheel in its pivoted fork. On top went a single seat and at the front leading link forks and an extensive mudguard. A shield covered much of the engine and ran forward to form legshields. The machine was sold as the Kawasaki Pet.

In the middle of 1961 Kawasaki Auto Sales was formed to sell the machines, and then in 1962 came the first motorcycle, the B8, to carry the Kawasaki badge. This was a 125 cc single like the B7 but with a revised engine design, transmission moved to the left side and the machine fitted with telescopic forks. It was joined by the B53 which was a variant of the M5 with the engine bored out to 55 cc.

That same year Meguro changed its name to Kawasaki Meguro and this was merged with Kawasaki Aircraft in 1963. The step-through range was expanded with the basic machine becoming the M5K and the larger 55 cc version the B55K, both fitted with a kickstarter and accompanied by the M5NC which had a centrifugal clutch.

During that year the firm took its first look at competition as a means of advertizing the name and chose the rather sluggish and underpowered B8 as the vehicle to work on. As they were still committed only to a home market they had no need to become involved with the European classic scene where their fellow Japanese firms were engaged in tremendous struggles between themselves and with the Italian factories.

Instead they turned to the Japan motocross championships, developed the B8, painted the tanks red and took the first six places in the 125 cc class. Immediately they had something to shout about and an identification at the circuits as the 'Red Tank Kawasaki'. It was a promotion point they were to remember well and use with great effect in later years.

Kawasaki came into the market very late in the day after the traumatic commercial battles of the fifties and at a time when the industry in Japan was reaching maturity. They lacked the others' years of experience and background, although Meguro helped to fill in many of the gaps, but had the financial resources to think big. Also they had to move that way as they would only be competitive by producing in volume and only volume would create the cash flow to keep the main board interested.

So with the home market satisfied, and down to replacement needs, and machines that had reached an acceptable level of technical sophistication and reliability, all the Japanese firms were looking to an export market world wide. Kawasaki started in this direction in a modest way in 1964 by exporting the B8 to the USA and setting up a branch office in Los Angeles to research the market in the Western USA.

In 1965 they opened another branch office, this time in Chicago to look at the Eastern half of the country and continued with the 125 which they sold as the 'Omega' with limited success. So they pulled out and thought about selling in America and came to the conclusion that machines developed for utility use in Japan had no real sale in the USA. What was needed was to look at the market, hire an American staff, listen to them and then build what the public wanted to buy.

So they did just that.

2 Early babies and single cycles

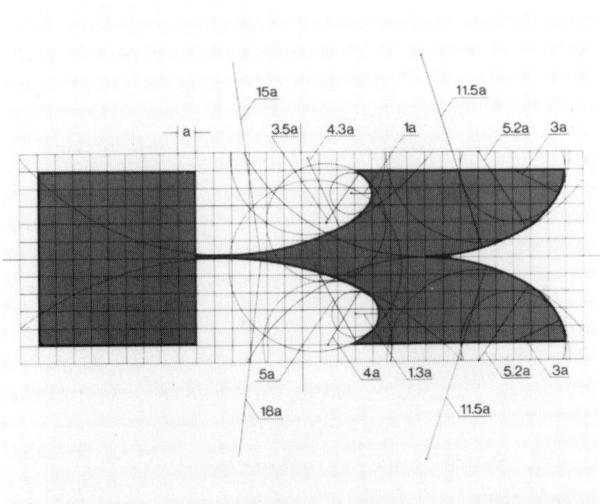

The Kawasaki 'big K' logo is a carefully proportioned form and the company book laid this down very exactly. Woe betide anyone who mistreated it

The first motorcycle to carry the Kawasaki name was the B8, and outside Japan it had nothing to make it memorable. It was a typical utility machine of its era, well built, tractable and pleasant enough to ride but with nothing to distinguish it from the next.

The B8 had a single cylinder engine of conventional two-stroke design built in unit with a four-speed gearbox. Maximum power was quoted as 11 bhp at 6000 rpm but the early models were less fiery and made do with 8. The final drive was on the left as was the rocking pedal gear lever, and the rear chain was fully enclosed.

The frame was typical of the time with a pressed steel backbone spine that ran from headstock to rear units and extended down behind the engine unit to support it and the rear fork pivot. A tubular brace ran from the headstock to the front of the crankcase with welded on plates bolting to the engine. The space inside the frame was put to use to accommodate battery, indicator relay, wiring and tools with access via large covers on each side. A further cover shrouded the carburettor to give a clean line to the engine and a well valanced mudguard tail was joined to the main frame.

The front forks were telescopics and carried a deeply valanced mudguard supported by a pair of stays on each side. Both wheels had wire spokes and drum brakes with a tyre size of 3·00 × 16 inch.

The headlight was held in a nacelle which also

Above **The 250 cc SGT touring single**
Top **85 cc J1 built from 1965–68**
Left above **First competition model, the B8M**
Left top **First Kawasaki motorcycle, the B8**

carried the speedometer, and both the nacelle and the fuel tank had the chunky Japanese style then current. The tank contained petrol-oil mix, or petroil, as no oil pump was fitted to that engine, and carried kneegrips and small round tank badges.

A single seat sat on the frame with a rear carrier behind it with passenger hand grip at its front end. Pillion footrests were provided mounted on the rear fork, and the ends of the fork were carried up to meet the short rear units.

Along with the B8 came the various 50 and 55 cc step-throughs, and in 1964 two more versions of the larger model appeared. The first was a simple bore job on the B8 to produce the B8S of 150 cc and a little more power. In other respects it copied the smaller model but was fitted with a full dual-seat in place of the single pad and carrier. In addition it was available in a number of colours and not just the black of the B8.

The second model was the B8T which was considered to be a touring model and this designation reflected the condition of the roads outside towns in that part of the world. Because they were dust tracks and paths in the main, a machine intended to travel between towns and villages rather than just commute in cities required to be built more to the modern trail format. So the B8T had trail tyres and a sprung front mudguard blade mounted well clear of the wheel. A single seat was fitted along with a rear carrier, the rear mudguard was slightly shortened and the rear units lost the covers over the springs to allow them to cool off more easily. Finally, an open rear chain was used with just a small guard over the top run.

The B8 and its variants ran on to 1966 and were joined in 1965 by a dual purpose version typed the B8TR of 125 cc. In that year the range expanded with two 50s and a whole series based on an 85 cc two-stroke engine all using the same frame and basic cycle parts.

The smaller models were the M10 of 50 cc and the M11 which had a slightly enlarged capacity of 52 cc thanks to a 1 mm greater bore. Both were otherwise very similar with the single cylinder two-stroke engine built in unit with the three-speed gearbox. The cylinder was inclined nearly to the horizontal and topped by a well finned head. The normal three ports were used with a long inlet tract bent down to bring the carburettor near level, and it connected to an air cleaner set in the body of the frame.

The cycle parts followed the lines set by the B8 with a spine frame extended back to form the rear mudguard and down to carry the engine unit and rear fork. A thin tie rod ran from the back of the barrel up to the headstock to brace the motor. The rear fork was built up from pressings and telescopics went on the front. Wheels were wire, brakes drum and tyre sections narrow at 2·25 in. on 17 in. rims. The M10 was fitted with a dualseat, while the M11 had a single and a carrier and both models were available in a choice of red or black.

The road versions of the 85 cc machine numbered five in all, two of which were touring models but this definition had already changed. It now brought an upswept exhaust and whitewall tyres although it kept the open rear chainguard in place of the usual chaincase. What had been a tourer for the B8 series now became trail machines and there were two of these in addition to the road models.

The engine unit for this series was an 85 cc two-stroke single with a rotary disc inlet valve and the first Kawasaki model to be fitted with this system. The cylinder was inclined forward only a little and this brought it much closer to the front of the frame pressings than on the 50. The space left was used to accommodate the

The 85 cc J1T model, a touring version of the J1 also available with engine oil pump

air filter trunking and this led down to the right side of the engine where the carburettor and disc valve were situated. As on the 50, the exhaust came from the front of the barrel and swept along the right side low down to the silencer.

In other respects the machines were as the 50s with the basic model, the J1, having a single seat and carrier while others had the dualseat. The two other road machines were the J1D which had an electric starter and the J1L which had an oil pump and so did away with the need to mix petroil. The two tourers were the J1T and the J1TL with the oil pump and both had the exhaust pipe curled up to run along high up on the right with a long slotted heat shield attached to it. The tyres had whitewall sides, only a chainguard was fitted for the rear chain, and a carrier went behind the dualseat.

The J1 series represented several technical strides forward for Kawasaki as in one range they introduced the disc valve, electric starting and an oil pump, although no model had all three items. It was a clear indication that they meant business and intended to move forward in the forefront leaving basic designs to others.

In the autumn the firm announced a second series of models, this time of 125 cc and intended to replace the B8, already viewed as becoming obsolete. The new machines used the coding B1 and, like the J1, were built in a number of forms. These were the basic B1, the B1L with oil pump, the B1T basic tourer and B1TL tourer with oil pump.

As a basic, no-nonsense commuter, it was to have a very long production run with remarkably few changes. It was sold everywhere except North America, although in its final years it was restrited to South America, the Middle East region and Africa. As the B1L series it ran to 1976 when it was renamed the KC125 and continued in that form to 1980. First and last models use the same workshop manual and, badges and insignia aside, the differences are minimal.

The B1 was developed from the B8 and followed the same format except for the adoption of a disc inlet valve. Otherwise it was the same layout with single cylinder, four-speed gearbox, spine frame, telescopics and drum brakes. The styling was more rounded with separate headlamp shell and the machine had the normal Japanese full range of ancillaries such as mirror and indicators.

The two tourers followed the same theme as the 85 cc models with upswept and shielded exhaust system, white lines running round the tyre walls, chainguard and no spring covers on the rear units. Again, as on the smaller models, the front forks were fitted with gaiters.

While the variants of the B1 appeared in August 1965, it was not until December that the base model itself was launched and it was preceded by a larger model, the 175 cc F1, which

was announced in October. This was in effect a bored out version of the B8 so it retained the three port type engine of that machine but did have the added attraction of an electric starter. It was really only a stop-gap for April 1966 saw it replaced by the F2 which had a disc valve engine and copied the B1L including its oil pump.

The F2 had the front fork gaiters and the rear units without spring covers of the tourers along with the skimpy chainguard they fitted. Its headlamp shell followed a style of that period with a round tower set in its top to carry the speedometer and warning lights and this was in marked contrast to European lines which extended the shell to carry the instrument behind the light unit. The F2 carried the word 'Superlube' on its oil tank mounted on the right, for all the Japanese companies used some such term to describe their oil pump lubrication system on two-stroke engines with throttle control on the output. Whatever it was called it certainly made life easier for the rider and gave the engine a better time.

1966 also brought a second series in the 125 class, this being the 120 cc C1. This had a great deal in common with the B1 and like it was offered in basic form or as the C1D with electric start and C1L with an oil pump. Tank, kneegrips and front brake differed from the B1 as did the wheel size but in most other respects it was similar, although the power output was less. The three models were joined in 1967 by the C1DL which had both electric start and an oil pump, but all four were dropped late that year.

A smaller model was the D1, a 100 cc version of the B1T and J1T tourers with upswept exhaust and a white line on the tyre walls. The engine had a disc valve and produced the same power as the 120 cc C1. It was coupled to a four-speed gearbox and used the same narrow section tyres as the 120.

As well as the F2 there were also the B11L and B11TL which were enlarged, 175 cc, versions of the B1L and B1TL models and constructed on similar lines. At the same time the J1 series were revised to become the 90 cc G1 range, and these were very much as before although power was up a little. They were offered as the basic G1, the G1L with oil pump and the G1DL with pump and electric start which came along in 1967 with the G1M a moto-cross version to back up the trail model G1TRL that was also offered.

Early in 1967 the 120 cc C2SS went on offer

Left **1967–68 model C2SS of 120 cc and known as the Road Runner**

Right **175 cc Bushwhacker of 1968, the model F3, still reflects the Japanese touring image of poor inter-town roads** and was known as the 'Road Runner'. It was built in the style known in the USA as the street scrambler and was essentially to trail specification but with road tyres. Thus it had more ground clearance than the normal road model and the front down tube was tucked back to the crankcase much more to increase the clearance to the front wheel. The frame was a fully tubular cradle that fitted tightly round the engine unit and shortened the wheelbase to suit the off-road use. The exhaust was upswept on the right but the engine remained the usual disc valve single. Road tyres were fitted and road-style mudguards which were chrome plated, a change from the stainless steel used on some other models. It was not a long lived model only running into 1968.

In the middle of 1967 the M50 came along and this was a step-through on the lines of the Kawasaki Pet. Due to the high line of the centre shield it was more of a step-up-and-over, but otherwise mirrored the model type. It was driven by a 50 cc single cylinder, two-stroke engine coupled with a three-speed gearbox hung from a spine frame. Short leading link forks went at the front with the usual deeply valanced sprung mudguard. At the rear was a pivoted fork and full chaincase was provided to complete the enclosure of the machanics started by the combined engine and leg shields. A single saddle and rear carrier were fitted and the model came with mirror and turn indicators.

By this time Kawasaki had become established in the USA and were moving to larger capacities of road models for the country, while in the smaller sizes the trend was to trail and off-road machine types. This led to the introduction of the F3 at the start of 1968 this being a 175 cc model in street scrambler style called the 'Bushwhacker'. Like the C2SS, it retained road tyres and a close fitting front mudguard but in other respects was a trail bike. As with the 120, it had a tubular frame and conventional cycle parts.

Both the F2 and F3 were really intermediate models that fitted a need at the time for

machines that looked like trail bikes but which were more suited to road use. In time they developed into true off-road forms to trail, enduro and motocross specification while the road versions lapsed, the F2 in 1969 and the F3 in 1970. This was the end of such two-stroke singles in the Kawasaki range, although the smaller capacities up to 125 cc continued in many forms. This gave the company a firm home base and a good range to export into the Asian markets close to them, as well as further afield. Such a base was necess-

Above **The 90 cc GA2A with disc valve and five-speed box as built from 1971 to 1974**

Left **Earlier version, the GA2 with gaitered front fork, 1969 to 1970**

ary to gear up the factory for mass-production and pave the way to bigger capacity road models in a different form and style to the simple single.

1968 saw the introduction of no less than four new 90 cc machines all using the same basic engine and cycle parts. The engine unit followed the lines of the earlier G1 with a single cylinder inclined forward a little and carrying a well finned alloy head with central plug. A disc inlet valve was retained with the carburettor on the right and the air filter set in the top of the crankcase and connected via internal trunking.

The gearbox was built in unit with the engine and provided four speeds in the case of the GA1 and five for the other models. The gear pedal went on the left and a heel-and-toe lever was fitted to the more touring models. The kickstarter with folding pedal went on the right with the rear brake pedal. Final drive went on the left with the chain fully enclosed by a case on the GA1 only.

All four machines had the engine unit installed in a tubular cradle frame with duplex down tubes between which the exhaust pipe ran. Suspension was by telescopics and pivoted fork and, while all the front forks were gaitered, the rear units varied regarding spring covers although all were the De Carbon type with sealed in nitrogen gas. Thus the GA1 had covers as did the GA2 which was very similar aside from the extra gearbox

ratio, chainguard and colour finish in place of the black.

The wheels had wire spokes, drum brakes and 18 in. rims, while tyre sections were 2·50 or 2·75 in. Mudguards were stainless steel and of sports section and all models were fitted with a dualseat, separate headlamp shell, full lighting equipment and instruments.

Differences were small. The basic model was the GA1 built for road use. Fitted with a five-speed gearbox it became the GA2, and these two models carried side cover logos of '90S' and '90SS' respectively. The third machine was a street scrambler version of the second and typed the GA3 while it carried a logo reading '90SSS'. It had its exhaust swept up to run along on the left with a heat-shield clipped to it, unlike the other models who wore their systems low down on the right. The GA3 had a universal front tyre but retained the close fitting mudguard, while at the rear the guard was cut short and the tail light high mounted.

The fourth model was the G3SS and this shared a common fuel tank with the GA3 that had a deeper front section and carried the marque name in block letters. It also lacked kneegrips which remained on the other tanks along with chrome side panels and plastic name badges. The power output of the G3SS was a little down on the other three models, possibly because it carried a more massive silencer and this was the only one of the four that was sold in the USA. It was finished in pastel and candy blue for the tank, while the GA3 was in pastel orange.

Further versions were built for Japan only in 1969 these being the GA0 which used the four-speed engine, and the GA4 which was an improved GA3. In their home country these were marketed as the '90' and '90-TR' respectively. These were followed late in 1970 by the GA5 which was an improved version of the GA2.

It was also slightly larger at 100 cc and of rather different design although the basics were very similar. Thus while the engine followed the same layout with inclined cylinder and disc valve inlet, the air filter became a round drum mounted behind the barrel. It used the five-speed gearbox and full rear chaincase while the final transmission remained on the left.

The frame was the tubular cradle with twin down loops and the front forks and rear units both had spring covers. In other respects it continued as a small capacity commuter machine with full equipment and instruments and able to carry rider and passenger. It was sold world wide except for North America.

It was about this time that Kawasaki began to identify their models by varying the type number each year. Not every machine followed this style and some continued with the basic typing for several years, but others would be given a suffix letter which changed annually. In later years an alpha-numeric suffix came into use so that as well as A, B, C, etc., they used A1, A2 and then maybe B1 to signify a more major change.

Early examples of this came in 1971 with the 90 cc models. Thus appeared the GA1A which continued with the four-speed engine unit but received a new seat and a deeper tank with new graphics on it and the side panels. It was also fitted with forks with spring covers and without gaiters and all these changes repeated themselves on the GA2A which was also fitted with rear units less spring covers.

In the same way came the G3SSA with new tank and larger side covers both with new logos and a change of paint. Mechanically the models were left alone and for all the variety of model names and numbers Kawasaki kept building the same basic units for a long time. This gave them and their dealers good continuity, easy spares stocking and enabled many of the cycle parts to interchange in fitting if not in aesthetics.

1972 brought the G3SSB with another tank, another colour and revised markings, while a

Left **Japanese advert (in English!) for the GA5A, a 100 cc development from the smaller GA2A**

Right **1974 G3SSD, another variant on the 90 cc disc valve design**

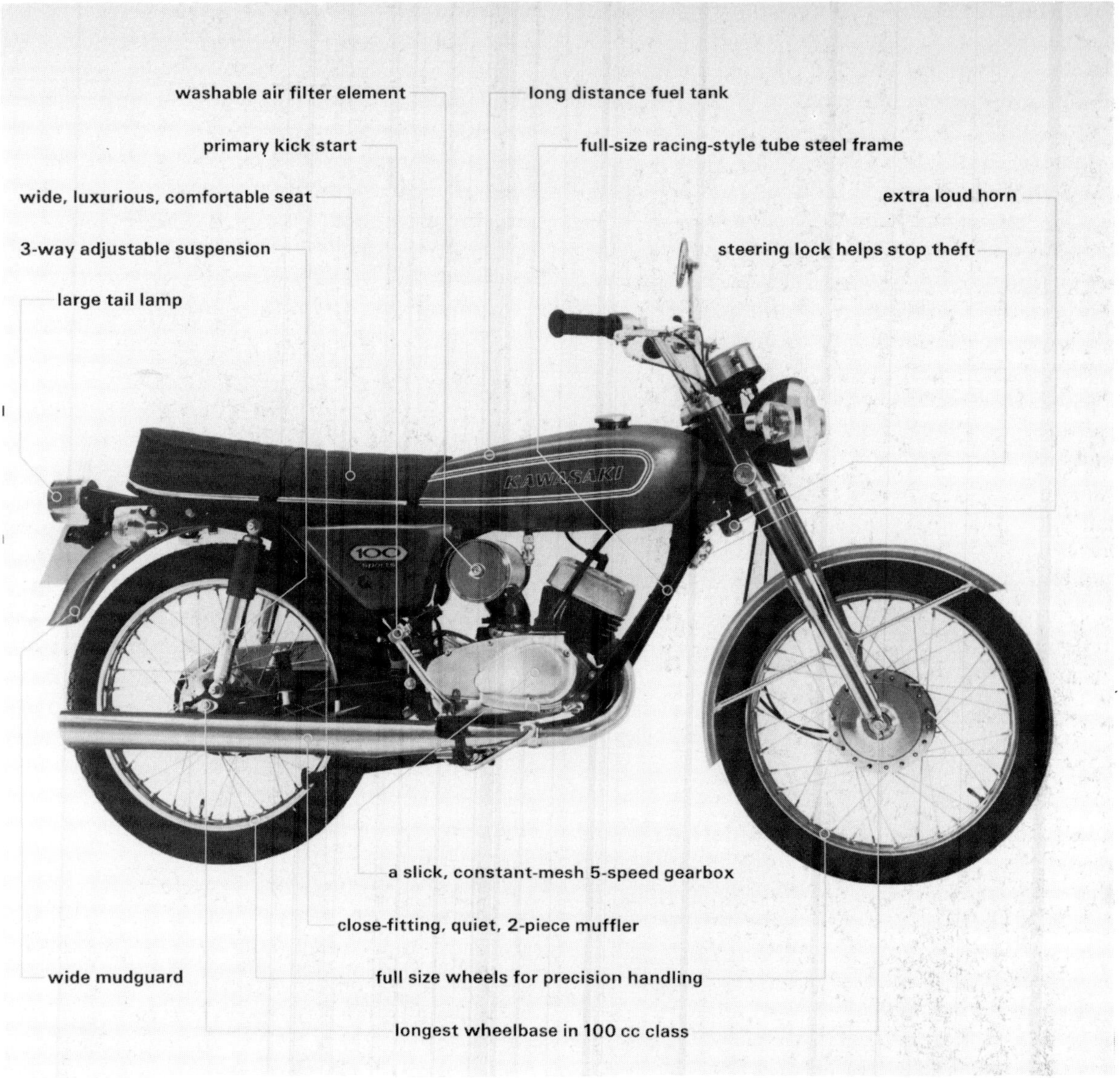

Above **Sales manual picture of 1974 G7T using 100 cc disc valve engine. G7S very similar except four speeds in place of five**

Right **Later G7TA produced in 1975 and 1976, 100 cc and five speeds, which became the KH100 series**

new 100 cc model was the G7T. Its engine was much as the 90 and it retained the disc inlet valve but the side cover was different and the air cleaner went into a cylindrical container mounted across the frame above the gearbox. A rubber hose connected it to the crankcase and cast-in tracts led to the carburettor. The model had the five-speed gearbox and the power unit was mounted in a new tubular cradle frame with duplex down tubes. Equipment was to full street standard with dualseat, indicators and instruments and with a sleek tank the machine looked much more the part than the earlier models.

The G7T was joined by the G7S early in 1973 and this was a near replica even to the colours available, except for the transmission. It had to manage with the four-speeds only and so the gearing was altered to suit. These two models were repeated in the 90 cc size for the home market as the G8T and G8S with five- and four-speeds and marketed in Japan as the '90-SS' and '90-DX' respectively.

Abroad 1973 brought the G3SSC with yet another change in colour and markings along with an air cleaner as used on the GA5, this vertical drum being a popular style for a number of Kawasaki models. The machine also had the seat altered in appearance by a change to the piping.

New models during the year were the G2T and G2S with five- and four-speeds respectively and developed from the GA series. They both used the 90 cc engine with the drum style of air cleaner and were built as tourers with full chaincase and covers over the suspension springs. The G2S was only built up to the end of 1974 and only exported into South-East Asia and Africa so was a really basic model for such territories.

The G2T lasted longer, up to 1976, and then became the KC90 while it was sold into a much larger market, but not in North America or the South Pacific.

Five 90 cc models ran on in 1974, these being the GA1A, GA2A, G2S, G2T and the G3SSD. The last was the only one sold in North America so

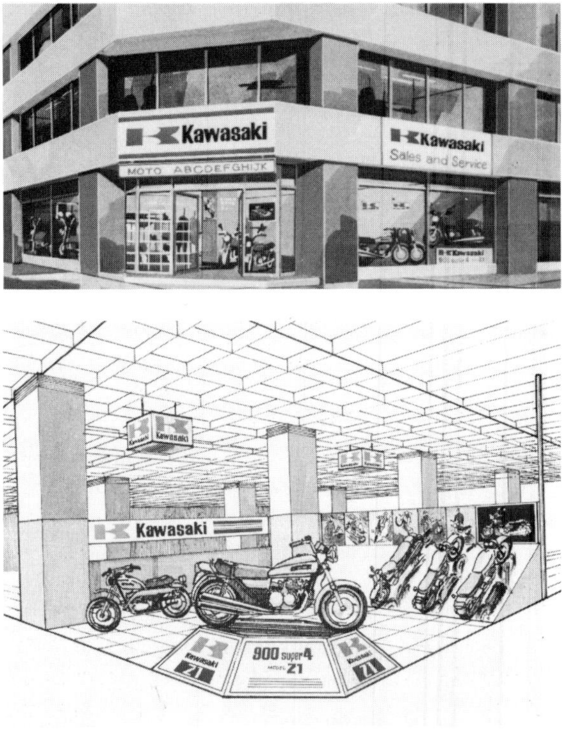

Taken from the sales manual issued by Kawasaki UK in 1974, these two drawings show a suggested shop front and interior for a solus dealer. Note Z1 featured in centre

it received the virtually obligatory colour and marking changes for the season. In addition, the tank was new as were the side covers, the rear mudguard was much shorter, a brake lining wear indicator was added and the front tyre section reduced slightly.

The 90s were accompanied by the venerable B1 which was still going strong and four 100 cc models. Of these the GA5A, G7T and G7S were as before but the G3T was new. This was built for South-East Asia only with the five-speed engine with drum air cleaner in a frame similar to that used for some of the 90s. The specification was much as the G2T with enclosure and full lighting and instrumentation.

For 1975 most of the 90s were dropped, only the G2T continuing, while one grew a little to become a 100. This was the G3SSE which was bored out 2·5 mm to increase the capacity and raise its power a little. The colour and markings were changed and at the front a kill-switch and front brake stop-light switch were added. In addition late in the year the tyre sections were increased to 2·75 in. front and 3·00 in. rear, although the wheel size remained at 18 in.

The G7S became the G7SA with a change of marking only as the four available colours continued. Electrically it altered by losing the charge rate switch and precisely the same changes produced the G7TA. Both the B1 and the G3T continued as they were.

1976 was the last year that Kawasaki kept to its letter series for the various models as it had used them since 1961 and the B7. Most had been changed at the end of 1975 but four small singles kept to the old style for one further year. After that they adopted a sequence of the letter K followed by a letter to indicate machine use, then the capacity and finally the series suffix.

The four were the G2T, G7TA, G3T and faithful B1, and all were to be renumbered in the new style for 1977. Thus they became the KC90, KH100, KH100-C and KC125, the last still very much as the B1L of a decade before and still sold in most countries.

From the B, C, D, F, G, J and M models came a new generation of lightweight Kawasaki motorcycles to make their mark on the road, to commute, to carry their riders out and about, and to continue the work done by their predecessors.

3 Early in the field

The 1966 175 cc F1TR, a trail version of the road F1 with piston controlled induction. A true trail bike with sump plate, it also had dual range sprockets and electric start

Kawasaki's roots in the off-road area go back to their early days when they built and raced the Red Tank models so successfully in Japan in 1963. From that early effort came a long stream of machines of all sizes and built for all the many forms of riding away from tarmac. They ranged from the most simple of trail machines which would seldom see a path to out-and-out motocross models able to run with the best in international competition. There were some odd models for special jobs and even miniatures that folded up for transport.

The first result of the Japanese success in 1963 was the 125 cc B8M. This was a pure motocross machine with the four-speed, 125 cc engine of the road model modified to push the power up. It retained the carburettor behind the barrel and piston controlled inlet while on the exhaust side a high level system was used.

The frame was the spine one minus the side covers with a short rear mudguard extending from the body. Telescopic forks were fitted along with standard wheels shod with competition tyres. The front mudguard was sprung and thus well clear of the wheel and both hubs were of the full width type with drum brakes. An open chainguard protecting the top run only went in place of the chaincase but tank and seat were stock B8. The rear dampers lost their spring covers, braced bars were fitted and the footrests were substantial and mounted from the frame under the engine unit. As on the road model,

the engine was supported in the frame by a down tube connecting headstock to crankcase.

The B8M was introduced in October 1963 and was joined in February 1965 by the B8TR which was a dual purpose model combining features from both road and motocross to give a trail bike. That same year also saw the appearance of a trio of 85 cc models based on the J1 road machine. These were the J1TR trial model, the J1TRL with oil pump, and the J1M motocross machine. All used the same four-speed engine unit and spine frame with the exhaust of the trail bikes upswept with a heat shield as on the road J1T version. Unlike that machine they also had a skid plate fitted beneath the engine, competition tyres and a sprung mudguard, although the rear one continued with its deep valance just as on the J1. The trail machines were fully equipped with lights, instruments, a mirror and rear carrier, while the motocross model was fully stripped.

In the same way the 175 cc F1TR was based on the road model F1, itself an enlarged B8. It managed to look a very business-like machine with the exhaust upswept on the right with its heat shield, short sprung front mudguard with ample clearance and competition tyres. It developed no more power than the road model and used the same spine frame with added down tube brace but did have a skid plate and dual sprockets with easy change to give it four high or low ratios. It also retained its electric starter which made it something of a novelty among small trail machines. To suit that use it shed its pillion footrests, was fitted with a single seat only, and had a substantial rear carrier bolted above the rear mudguard.

Above **An early motocross model, the 250 cc F21M built from 1968 to 1970. Quick, but in need of chassis development**

Right **The 120 cc Road Runner in C2TR trail bike form with knobbly tyres, sump plate, sprung mudguards and luggage carrier**

Both it and the J1 models continued for 1966 but were joined early that year by the F2TR which followed the same pattern but was based on the disc valve F2 model. It acquired the skid plate, tyres, exhaust and mudguard in the same manner as the F1 and in due course replaced it.

The middle of the year brought the B1M which was a motocross version of the B1, and late in the year came the F21M. This was Kawasaki's first model with a 250 cc single cylinder, two-stroke engine and it was based on the F2 engine opened up in size. It was a pure motocross model and as such unusual in that it retained the disc inlet valve and consequent engine width at crankcase level. An expansion box exhaust was fitted upswept on the left and, although this was tucked in an much as possible, it also carried a brief heat shield.

The frame was a tubular cradle with duplex tubes running from the headstock down and under the engine before turning up to join the single top tube. A light sub-frame supported the tops of the rear spring units, the brief mudguard and the short padded seat. The telescopics at the front lacked gaiters to protect the stanchions, which would have quickly become pitted under racing conditions with the inevitable loss of oil and damping that would have followed.

Finish was in lime green or candy red for the tank and this was the first appearance on a production model of the light green shade that was to become so associated with the competition Kawasaki in the years ahead, and from which they acquired their nickname of 'Green Meanies'.

The F21M was only sold in North America and it was joined in 1967 by two 120 cc models both sold with the 'Road Runner' name. The first was the C2SS already described, and built in street scrambler guise, while the second was the C2TR which was in the trail machine format. Thus it had a dual gear range to back up the four-speed gearbox, skid plate, trail tyres and small mudguards with plenty of clearance. The disc valve engine was retained complete with upswept exhaust pipe and the model was equipped with lights, stands and rear carrier.

It was joined by two 90 cc models based on the basic G1, the first the G1TRL trail model and the second the G1M for motocross. Both kept the spine frame of the road model and were equipped to suit their purpose, the G1M with an expansion chamber upswept on the left of the machine. That model also continued the Red Tank theme for its colour of that item and was fitted with stainless steel mudguards. Its power output was nearly double that of the road model and the engine ran up to 9000 rpm.

Along with these new models the 85 cc J1TR and 175 cc F2TR machines continued for 1967 with the 250 cc motocross one and the 90, 120 and 250 cc ones all ran on for 1968, while the 85s lapsed. The latter year saw the introduction in October of the 250 cc F4 trail model which was marketed in Japan as the 250-TR and elsewhere as the 'Sidewinder'.

Right **With prop stand mounting that is looking for a rock to remove it, the 1969–70 F4 Sidewinder with 250 cc disc valve engine**

Below **The larger 350 cc F5 Big Horn of 1970 with tucked in prop stand and Hatta fork. Also has CDI and alloy rims**

The F4 was similar to the F3 Bushwhacker but orientated to trail build. It used the 250 cc disc valve engine which breathed through an air cleaner set behind the barrel and exhausted into a silencer mounted high on the left just below the base of the tank and seat. A four-speed gearbox was built in unit with the engine and the final drive was on the left protected by a light guard.

The frame was a tubular cradle with duplex down tubes and fitted tightly round the engine unit to give it good protection and ample ground clearance. This last aspect was unfortunately rather reduced on the left by the prop stand which hung down ready to catch on the first rock that came along. The front forks carried the small front mudguard attached to the lower legs so it was unsprung and hugged close to the tyre more in street scrambler style than trail bike.

At the rear were De Carbon type gas units to control the pivoted fork and the wheels mirrored the motocross 250 in their diameters and sections. Thus the front was 3·25 × 19 in. and the rear 4·00 × 18 in., both with a trial universal tread pattern. The lights were quickly detachable so, aside from the front fender, the model was well equipped for serious trail riding in the prime USA market.

It was a period when the off-road US market was expanding. Americans had always tended to

Right side of the 1970 F5 showing installation of disc valve, diaphragm fuel tap and push-pull throttle cable

Above **1970 G31M Centurian, a 100 cc motocross version of the G3TR. Disc valve, five speeds and high level expansion box with tiny tailpipe**

Right **The 1971 F7, a dual purpose 175 cc model with Hatta fork and front mudguard flap. By turning fork legs three spindle positions are possible**

go for cubes and this reflected in their road bike preferences for the Harley and the large English twins. Then they discovered off-road riding and with large tracts of open country at their disposal it was soon the fun thing to do. They also quickly found that large, heavy road machines were not the best suited for the conditions and made for hard work. Rapidly it became preferred to have a light two-stroke which was fast enough to be interesting but light enough to allow the rider to have fun. It was also easy to hitch such a machine on to the back of a camper and go off for the weekend with plenty of home comforts.

Trail bikes became very popular and, while the English industry floundered with their restricted range of big twins, the Japanese firms (including Kawasaki) rushed to meet the demand for off-road machinery.

In addition to the Kawasaki models the F3 Bushwhacker also appeared in the USA under the American Eagle label. In this guise it was fitted with a different American made 'plastic' tank, had gaiters added to the front fork, a mainly black finish to the crankcase, larger side panels and new mudguards. These last were changed to a shorter one at the rear and sprung at the front to give ample clearance to the trail tyres.

Despite the patriotic naming, all the American Eagle machines came from lands far away for, in addition to the Japanese Kawasaki, they also sold the Italian Laverda and English Sprite, all with a badge decorated with the American national bird. It was a make that ran for a couple of years but finally lapsed through lack of money and thus machines as the Japanese established themselves with full back-up over the US scene.

1969 saw the two 250s, the F4 and F21M, continue along with the 90 cc G1TRL, but the G1M and C2TR were dropped. Three new models were introduced, two of 100 cc capacity and the third a new single cylinder size for the firm, 350 cc.

The first of these to appear, in March, was the G31M which was a 100 cc motocross model with five-speed disc valve engine tucked into a twin loop cradle frame. It carried its expansion chamber high on the left with a long, very small diameter tailpipe and was called the Centurian.

Next came the G4TR Trail Boss with a less highly tuned engine but still with five speeds and tucked in a very similar frame. This ran round the back of the gearbox and then up and forward as on the moto-crosser but carried extra equip-

The 350 cc F9 of 1972, a model developed from the earlier F5

Above **1973 G6, a five-speed 90 cc model sold in Japan as the 90-TR**

Right **The 250 cc F11, also from 1973, with new seat, marking and tailpipe extension for that year**

ment brackets and lacked the long headstock brace of the competition machine. It did have a dual gearbox range facility to give it a total of ten gears with a quick change from high to low.

The exhaust was high on the left, a skid plate went under the engine and the rear chain was protected by a rather skimpy guard with lightening holes in it. In addition to this a loop guard ran under the lower chain run just in front of the rear sprocket to clear any debris away from the chain as it ran onto the sprocket.

Both wheels had the same size 3·00 × 18 in. tyres and these were shielded by stainless mudguards. The seat was rather short for two but more than adequate for the single rider it was only really meant to carry, and behind it went a tubular luggage rack. Lighting equipment and a front wheel driven speedometer were provided and the prop stand was very well tucked away to lie just under the rear fork leg.

The big single was the 350 cc F5 which was called the 'Big Horn'. It mirrored the F4 in most respects but with the larger capacity engine and a five-speed gearbox. The disc inlet valve was used with the air cleaner lodged behind the cylinder, but ignition was electronic with a CDI system and there were other refinements such as a diaphragm fuel tap.

The frame was a duplex loop cradle type, not quite on the lines of the F4 and, as on the small G4TR, the prop stand was tucked out of harm's way and a chain protector loop fitted below the bottom run. At the front went Hatta forks but without gaiters. These were named after the Kawasaki engineer who designed them and had sliders machined at the lower end to take the wheel spindle in any of three positions. Thus by moving the wheel it was possible to alter the fork trail to suit different conditions. The idea was good but the forks tended to be a little flexible in use. Both wheels had aluminium alloy rims with the front of 21 in. diameter and this marked the first use of this size on a Kawasaki trail bike. At the rear went an 18 in. and this was turned by an aluminium sprocket.

Big Green Meanie, the 1973 F12MX of 450 cc with massive exhaust system and lots of horsepower. Rather special rear units

With 33 bhp available to push it along it was a fast machine for trail riding and must have given its owners some exciting times. It came in one colour for that year, which was Rawhide.

The G1TRL was the only machine that was dropped for 1970, the two 100s, two 250s and the 350 all continuing. They were joined by five further models with two new 250s to replace the existing ones, 125 and 175 cc versions of the trail bikes and a tiny 75 cc folding compact design.

This last, the MT1, appeared in the middle of the year and was designed to be carried in the boot of a car. To this end the handlebars could

Left side of the 1973 250 cc F11 with piston controlled inlet and moulded tail cover

be folded down to reduce the overall height and both petrol and oil tank vents could be shut to prevent leakage. The engine unit was a 75 cc single cylinder, two-stroke with piston controlled inlet. The barrel was well inclined with a detachable alloy head whose fins ran from top to bottom as did those on the cylinder. The carburettor with its air cleaner went to the rear on an inlet tract bent to bring it to be parallel to the ground, while the exhaust curled up sharply on the right to run along high up just below the tank and seat.

A three-speed gearbox with footchange pedal on the left was built in unit with the engine and driven via an automatic centrifugal clutch. A tiny kickstart lever went on the right with folding pedal and the final drive chain went on the left under a brief guard for the top run.

The engine unit went into a spine frame that ran back from the headstock and then down to mounting plates which held both the power unit and the rear fork pivot. These plates were continued down and forward under the gearbox to support the footrest bar and the prop stand on the left. The engine was also held by a tie-rod that joined the back of the barrel to the spine underside and a sub frame ran back and up to carry the seat, take the top mountings of the rear suspension units and form a lifting handle behind the seat.

Suspension was conventional, although the rear units, which were without spring covers, did look out of proportion to the machine. At the front went short telescopics with small external and exposed springs on each fork leg. The wheels were minute with well treaded tyres in the scooter size of 3·50 × 8 in. and were mounted on split rim wheels. Both were fitted with small drum brakes and both brakes were controlled by hand levers, there being no foot pedal.

The front mudguard was truly minimal being extremely abbreviated and mounted to the lower fork crown so well clear of the tyre. At the rear a guard sat above the wheel with the rear

The 1973 350 cc F9A with disc inlet and Hatta fork

light and a number plate hung from the rear frame loop. A small fuel tank and a seat completed the package which came equipped with lights but no instruments.

The other new models all came in May or June and the 125 cc F6 and 175 cc F7 were very similar and used a common frame. The F8 was the 250 cc machine which replaced the F4 and it was very similar to the F5 Bighorn with Hatta forks and alloy rear sprocket. It was sold as the 'Bison' in its markets in the Americas and the South Pacific, but went under the guise of the '250-TR' at home in Japan.

The F7 also had the Hatta fork and being aimed at on- and off-road use sported a flap at the tail of its front mudguard and a rear carrier. The F6 had a front fork whose length was adjustable and the same rear carrier plus a different pair of tyres. In most ways all the trail models, F5, F6, F7 and F8, followed the same format.

The final new machine was a motocross version of the F8, typed the F81M, which replaced the earlier F21M. It showed up the improvements and changes that had come in a few years with much trimmer lines, five-speed gearbox, bigger front wheel and tucked in details. Power output was given as being lower and at a slightly reduced engine speed which suggested that peaky output had been exchanged for a broader based spread of more use when racing.

Other than the superseded F4 and F21M, all the F series continued into 1971 in 125, 175, 250 and 350 cc sizes. Of these the largest became the F5A with changes in the colour which became lime green, to the marking and to the finish of the exhaust pipe heat shield. The others remained as they were. At the other end of the capacity scale the baby MT1 continued as it was, along with the G31M, but the other 100 cc model became the G4TRA by dint of colour and marking changes plus a chrome plated heat shield for the silencer.

Two new 100 cc models joined the line-up that year, one, the G3TRA, only to be produced for a few months. It was based on the 90 cc G3TR with the capacity increased by boring the barrel out. The extra size won it an extra horse-power and the machine's appearance was altered by

Above **Interesting special based on F9 engine and run at Daytona in 1973**

Right **The inimitable Don Smith on the trials prototype in 1973 which led to the production KT250 trials machine in 1975**

changes to colour, markings, fuel tank, side covers, silencer heat shield and front mudguard. This last became sprung so it was well clear of the tyre and also much shortened so no stays were needed to support it.

The second new 100 was the G5 which was a dual purpose, on- and off-road model fitted with universal tyres and not unlike the F6. It

retained the disc valve engine and five-speed gearbox and was fitted with a moulded cover or tail which ran from the seat to the rear lamp above the rear mudguard. Although a small model it was fitted with pillion footrests but the rear chainguard was cut very short as on nearly all the trail machines.

Of the larger new machines the first was the 350 cc F9 which came in April to replace the F5. It was a developed version of the earlier model so looked much like it as the lime green colour was continued, although the markings changed and the engine was finished in black. The power was down on that of the original Bighorn which suggested less but with a wider spread.

The final new model was the 250 cc F11 which appeared in July as a successor to the F8. Unlike the 350 this was a much more radical change as the disc valve was dropped and piston controlled induction used. This tucked the carburettor much more out of the way and allowed the engine to be narrowed down at the vital crankcase level. A five-speed gearbox was fitted and a substantial plate went under the front of the engine unit attached to the twin down tubes of the loop cradle frame. In other respects the cycle side was much as its predecessor but it did have alloy wheel rims fitted and also a moulded tail cover as the G5. Although a trail bike, it was fitted with turn indicators in addition to full lighting equipment so could be used on the road, on trails or even in enduros.

In addition to the short lived G3TRA, the G31M, F81M and F5 were all left out of the 1972 range. This had the G5, F9 and F11 continuing as they were, while the others changed their coding. This gave the MT1A and in addition to colour and marking changes this model also had its front forks modified so the springs were fitted internally which cleaned up the looks a good deal.

On the G4TRB the colour and markings changed and the quick change lever for the dual range gearbox was moved onto the right handlebar. The F series had colour and marking changes with the addition of an emblem on the oil tank, '125' for the F6A, and '175' for the F7A. For the F8 it was a marking change only as the colours remained the same.

New models were the G6, a five-speed 90 sold in Japan as the '90-TR', and the 250 cc F11M introduced in July. This was a moto-cross version

Above **Richard Sunter riding in the Hoad trial late in 1973 on the 250 cc Kawasaki prototype trials iron**

Right **The 1974 KS125 which was developed from the earlier F6 series. It retained the disc valve but added one gear to make six in all**

Rather special trials machine developed by Bob Gollner using the Kawasaki engine. Front fork and strange brake lever are stock KT250

of the trail F11 and only built in limited numbers for a short period. It had the power of the engine boosted but retained the piston controlled inlet with carburettor fed from an air box under the seat. Unlike the trail bike, the expansion chamber was run under the engine unit to turn up along the line of the sub frame to the tail pipe at the rear of the seat.

The frame was a duplex loop in chrome molybdenum steel, while the fuel tank was plastic with the filler cap fitted well forward and high up to reduce the chance of spillage. The general finish was black which applied to the engine and hubs in addition to the more usual areas of frame and seat, while the tank was in lime green. It was designed for serious work, looked the part, and only sold in North America.

The F11M continued to be offered for 1973 without change but the F11 which also ran on had its seat and markings altered and a tail piece added to its silencer. The other F series machines changed their suffix letter except for the F8A which was dropped. The F6B and F7B were given a new colour, a black finish to the engine, new markings and a change of tank and seat. In addition turn indicators were fitted as standard and

The Kawasaki Midi bike, the MC1, this one the B model from 1975 with usual 14 in. rear tyre. 90 cc disc valve engine and five speeds

the 175 fitted with a different grade of sparking plug. The 350 cc model became the F9A and again was fitted as standard with turn indicators, while its marking style altered.

Among the small capacity models, the MT1A had a change of colour only but the two 100 cc models both had this plus new markings and turn indicators as standard. The G4TRC, as one became, also had the cylinder and head painted black and a steering lock added, while the G5A, as the other was coded, had the front tyre diameter increased to 19 in.

Three new models were added to the existing 1973 range and the first came in January to represent a new type of model referred to as the 'Midi' bike. This was of a physical size to suit older children but also able to carry an adult on- or off-road without the constriction of the MT1 series. The new machine was the MC1 and marketed in Japan as the KM90.

It used a 90 cc single cylinder engine with disc inlet coupled with a five-speed gearbox. A high level exhaust was tucked into the left side with a heat shield and both items finished in black. The format was trail bike but on a reduced scale so that the engine unit was a tight fit in the frame despite its small size and the whole machine was in proportion.

Frame and suspension were conventional telescopics and pivoted fork but the wheels were of a size to match the rest of the model. The front was 16 in. diameter with a 2·50 in. section tyre, while the rear was only 14 in. diameter but had a fat, by its standards, 2·75 in. section. The usual fittings in the form of skid plate, small mudguards kept well clear of the wheels, prop stand only plus lights and indicators were provided and made for a neat and long running machine.

It was joined in July by the MC1M which was a moto-cross version with competition tyres,

When monkey bikes were to lose that name and become just 'mini bikes', Kawasaki produced the 73 cc MT1B in 1974

braced bars, racing plate and minus lights. Power output was the same as the trail machine and nearly all the fittings were the same to provide a neat machine for junior riders.

The third new model for 1973 appeared in February and while it was another motocross machine, it was at the other end of the spectrum to the MC1M. The model was the F12MX of 450 cc and a full blooded, international class competitor that called for a top level rider to use its 38 horses to the best advantage.

The single cylinder sat close to the vertical and breathed its mixture in via a piston controlled port so the carburettor was tucked in behind the barrel. The exhaust ran down from the port and under the engine and gearbox before emerging on the right with the remainder of the expansion box running up behind the sub frame tube to a horizontal outlet just below mudguard level. The relatively low peak engine speed of 5500 rpm called for a long and large chamber to suit the gas resonance and the size led to this installation problem.

The engine was in unit with a five-speed gearbox and was fired by a CDI system. The frame was a loop cradle with a single down tube and suspension by telescopics and pivoted fork. Equipment was normal motocross with competition tyres, braced bars, special rear damper units and a well tucked away air filter. In all the model had much in common with the 250 cc F11M.

Both went from the lists in 1974 although the larger did become the KX450 and in the same manner the F6B changed to the six-speed KS125. Of the remaining models, the MC1M remained unaltered but all the others changed their suffix letters.

The baby of the range became the MT1B and was fitted with a longer front mudguard to replace the very short one it had used up till then. It also had colour and marking changes and this applied to all the other models except the G5B which changed the marking only.

The MC1A had a revised seat with flip-up lever, a new left engine cover which extended to cover the final drive chain a little more, and brake wear indicators added. The G4TRD had its rear chainguard shortened, a new fuel tank and a '100' logo fixed to the silencer heat shield. The G5B had the brake wear indicators added, as did the F11A and F9B. The latter was fitted with the F11 type of front fork and a tail piece in the end of the silencer. The F7C had its silencer modified in this way plus revised tank, seat and tail light, while the other change on the F11A was to the engine covers which were no longer painted black.

New for 1974 was the 100 cc G4TRA which was not to be confused with the A version of the G4TR built in 1971. When seen there was no chance of any confusion for the new machine, also called the 'Agi Bike', was of a unique appearance and first built for the wide stock farms of Australia. Later it was sold elsewhere in the South Pacific and in Africa and Central and South America.

It was essentially a trail bike adapted for use in the outback and its most noticeable feature was the provision of a large spade mounted in a carrier on the right. It was based on the normal G4TR but had protection bars added to prevent immobilization from a minor spill far from home, a very real danger on the immense farms it was intended for.

Thus small crash bars were bolted across the lower part of the front down tube to protect the engine, exhaust system and rider's feet. A further cage went round the headlamp and instruments and a third fixed under the full chaincase to protect that item from occasional rocks. A carrier went behind the dualseat and the handlebar brace was extended out to protect the control levers if the machine fell over.

With its spade sticking out at the back it made an odd sight, but was well fitted out for its intended job.

1975 was the last year for the old style model coding for the trail type machines and by then many of the newer range were using the K sequence. Thus the older models only received a face lift in the main with colour and marking changes only to the G4TRE, G4TRAA, F7D, F11B and F9C. The MC1M changed its marking only, while the remaining models had minor mechanical alterations in addition to the colour and marking ones to go with their new suffix letters.

The MT1C had the front brake altered so that the backplate was on the right instead of the left, where it had been since 1970. The MC1B changed the rear tyre section to 3·00 in. and the G5C had the choke lever moved off the left switchgear assembly.

At the end of 1975 the MC1M and F9 were dropped but five models continued with a model name change and detail alterations. The MT1 became the KV75, the MC1 the KM90, and the G4TR in trail and Agi Bike forms became the KV100 but with suffixes of A7 and B2 to distinguish one from the other. Rather sadly the spade was no longer supplied so that unusual feature was lost, but a dual range ten-speed gearbox was adopted. The G5 became the KE100 and all models had suffix letters and numbers. The two F models were replaced by the KE175 and KE250 but these both received some re-design and became a new series. Over the years all the newer machines evolved further with new machines appearing such as the KT types built for trials and developed by Don Smith in Europe from 1972 onwards.

Thus Kawasaki continued to be active in the off-road field just as on the tarmac.

4 Banger singles and big twin copies

The W1 650 cc twin as built from 1966 to 1968 and derived from the older Meguro models themselves taken from the BSA twin A7 series

Kawasaki had placed a tentative toe in the large American market as early as 1964 but had limited success with their small two-stroke single sold as the Omega. They had entered a field of commercial competition totally different to their home one and found themselves face to face with opposition they had never dreamed of.

There were all their old friends from the homeland with such firms as Marusho with their BMW copies, Bridgestone, Lilac and the big three. There were the traditional big twins from England, BSA, Triumph, Norton and Enfield, and the smaller capacity Greeves and Cotton; even the big Panther and Velocette singles. From Europe there were Bultaco, Ducati, BMW, Lube, Parilla, Garelli, Vespa and Gilera along with US products such as the Harley and miniatures using all types of odd engines.

There was certainly plenty of opposition and a commuter 125 made a nil impact on the scene so the firm retired in some confusion to think about the American market. During this process they had a good look at the old Meguro range and the first result was some re-vamping of a couple of models from it. It also led to a blind alley where they lost their way for a short while.

The first rehashed Meguro was the SGT which appeared in September 1964, the year the first Los Angeles office was opened. It had a 250 cc single cylinder engine with overhead valves and was based on the Meguro S8, one of a series of such singles. The engine was built in unit with

The real original, a BSA A10 Golden Flash adapted by the Swedish police for their arctic conditions with skis and handchange. A feature not copied in Japan

the 4-speed gearbox and its iron cylinder was inclined very slightly forward and topped by an alloy head with fully enclosed valves and rockers.

Bore and stroke were the traditional BSA twin dimensions of 66 × 72·6 mm and the compression ratio was 8·7:1. Valve gear was simple with the camshaft set in the timing chest on the right side of the crankcase and above the crankshaft which drove it. The push rods moved in tunnels cast in the head and barrel with an access plate in the side of the rocker box. The points for the coil ignition were controlled by a cam which was driven from the end of the camshaft along with the auto-advance mechanism and were enclosed by a small circular cover.

A VM24H carburettor supplied the mixture and was connected to an air cleaner. The exhaust ran down to a low mounted silencer on the right and was held to the engine by a finned clip. The generator went on the crankshaft end and an electric starter was bolted to the front of the crankcase. Lubrication was wet sump with 2 litres of oil looking after engine, gearbox and primary transmission.

The 4-speed gearbox had both gear pedal and kickstart lever on the left and the rear chain was

Up in the hills with the W1SS in its 1968–71 form with twin carburettors, tuck-and-roll seat and short, stubby silencers

also on that side under a guard. In all it was a smooth contoured unit and the complete assembly went into a full loop cradle frame with pivoted fork rear suspension. At the front went telescopics and the handling was assisted by a steering damper.

The SGT was the touring version of the model and in line with the factory policy of those days was thus equipped with sports mudguards. It also had rather high bars with the grips laid back a trifle and a long deep tank with large kneegrips. A dualseat and pillion footrests were provided and the centre section of the machine had side covers under which went the tools, battery, electrical equipment and the air cleaner.

At the end of the year, in December, the SG was announced using the same basic engine unit, frame and forks with revised details. The wheels and hubs remained as they were with the latter full width and in light alloy to accommodate a pair of good sized single leading shoe brakes. The tyre diameters remained unchanged at 18 in. but the section reduced from 3·00 in. front and 3·25 in. rear to 2·75 and 3·00 in.

The fittings were less sporting with both mudguards well valanced and the rear number plate

support boxed in against the rear one. The bars were not quite so high although the grips were still laid back a touch and the side covers extended forward a little further but without enclosing the carburettor.

The seat was a single pan saddle pivoted at the nose with its support spring hidden from view and linked to work in cantilever fashion. This was a straight copy of the design used by many German machines and on the SG no pillion pad was provided although pillion footrests were fitted. A rear carrier went on top of the mudguard and a grab handle was bolted to its front.

Finally the tank shape was completely different and older fashioned. The tank was held by a single central bolt as on the BSA and Ariel at one time and had small kneegrips. The electrical equipment was just as comprehensive and included turn indicators.

The 250 single represented the tail end of the Meguro single line and ran on longer than expected to 1969 as a rather basic model but long before it was withdrawn it had been superseded by a 2-stroke powered machine of a different generation. It represented one of a series that were based on English designs and as such were rapidly left behind in the heat of the competition in Japan.

Another Meguro model that ran on as a Kawasaki appeared in March 1965 as the K2 twin. This was a doubled up 250 and a close copy of the 497 cc BSA A7 and had been built in the late fifties as the Meguro K1. With either badge on the tank it was a faithful replica of the English machine down to a copy of the Amal Monobloc carburettor. Detail differences amounted to the use of the same silencer style as on the SG and slightly altered lines but much of the mechanics were as on the mid-1950s BSA. Thus not only were the full width, light alloy, hubs retained but operation of the rear was as the BSA with the brake cross-rod running through the pivoted fork spindle from the left pedal to a cable connection on the right. The primary chaincase had the line of the BSA and a full rear chaincase was fitted as was optional on the Small Heath model.

The twin was very popular with the Japanese police so a model was introduced in May 1965 especially for them. To this end it was fitted with a single seat pad with a radio box behind it on a carrier, a siren, flashing blue lights and given an all white paint finish only relieved by the tank decor. It no doubt kept the Japanese road users in line.

In October 1965 the line of Kawasaki twins was joined by the W1 which was an enlarged version of the 500 cc model but which retained the BSA line to a great extent. The engine was a 360 degree parallel twin with overhead valves and working dimensions of 74 × 72·6 mm which gave a capacity of 624 cc. Compression ratio was 8·7 :1 and it produced 50 bhp at 6500 rpm.

As with its English counterpart, the engine was based on a vertically split light alloy crankcase with the timing chest built into the right case half and a small sump plate with oil strainer mesh bolted to its underside. A ball race supported the crankshaft on the timing side with a similar one on the drive side on some engines and a roller on others.

Unlike most English engines the Kawasaki used one piece connecting rods and needle bearing big ends. To enable these to be assembled the crankshaft was built up from three parts, two similar outer webs each forged complete with a mainshaft and a crankpin plus a central flywheel. This and the outer webs were formed to provide the desired balance factor and the parts were assembled by pressing the individual crankpins into a single hole bored through the flywheel.

Each rod was bushed at the small end and carried a conventional 4-stroke piston retained by circlips. The pistons had one scraper and two compression rings, the upper chrome plated, and were offset by a small amount to the rear.

They ran in a cast iron block held down on studs and this carried the four valve tappets each of which was retained by a guide pin. A single tunnel was cast into the rear of the block to accommodate the push rods. On top of the block went a one piece aluminium alloy head with cast-in valve inserts. It copied the BSA design down to having nine fixing bolts and repeated the two wells for the exhaust valves and single one for both inlets. Each valve was held to its seat by duplex springs retained by a collar and split collets and its guide was located by a circlip. The first head carried a single 31 mm carburettor feeding both cylinders but later models had twin

Left **Brochure for the W2SS or Commander model, 1968–70, developed engine with more power**

Below **W series crankshaft design with one piece rods, pressed assembly and all roller or ball bearings**

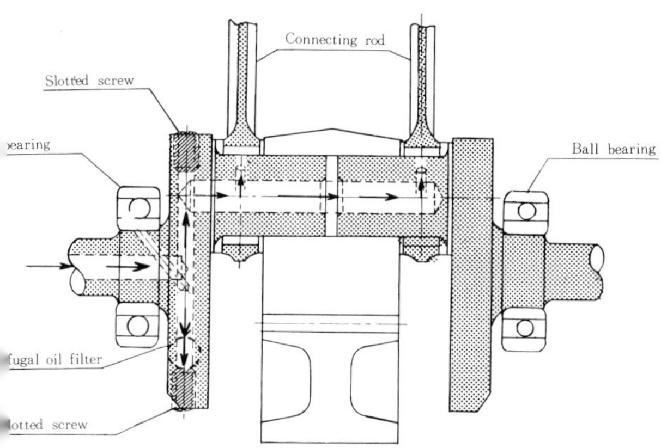

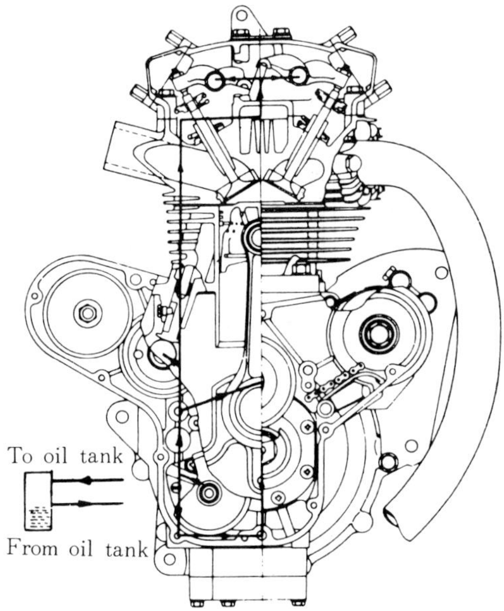

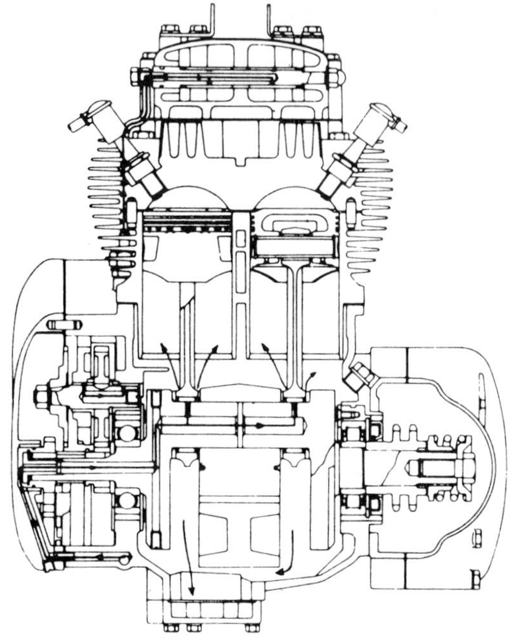

inlet ports and two 28 mm carburettors.

On top of the head went a one piece rocker box with two hollow rocker spindles each supporting two rockers. Each rocker had an adjuster at its outer end for setting the valve clearance and was moved by push rods constructed of steel tubing with ball bearings welded to each end. There were rocker covers above each pair of valves but no means of sighting the assembly of push rod ends into the rocker cups. Thus, just as with the BSA, a special guide plate was used to hold the push rods in the correct position as the rocker box was lowered into place.

The timing side was again BSA with a small gear on the crankshaft meshed with an idler which drove a gear on the end of the camshaft. This ran in bushes in the crankcase behind the crankshaft and its drive gear meshed with a further one behind it which drove the contact breaker cam and auto-advance unit. This sat behind the barrel and a single set of points was controlled by a twin lobe cam to fire both plugs from a double ended coil once every turn of the crankshaft. The idler gear shaft carried a sprocket and this was connected by chain to a dynamo clamped to the front of the crankcase. Unlike the BSA, the chain was tensioned by a slipper and was lubricated by the engine oil so did not have a separate compartment as did the greased BSA item.

The oil pump was of the internal rotor type and bolted to the wall of the timing chest where it was driven by a gear pair from the crankshaft end. As the engine had a dry sump lubrication system, the pump was a duplex one with feed and return elements protected by the sump filter and another in the oil tank. The oil supply to the bearings was into the crankshaft end to the big ends via drillings and by an external pipe to the rocker gear.

The timing gear was encased by a single outer cover bearing the Kawasaki name and the shape of this cover enhanced the BSA appearance. On the left the primary chaincase enclosed a duplex drive chain, an engine sprocket with cam type shock absorber and a multi-plate clutch

Left **Cross-section line drawings of W engine showing how similar it was to BSA. Later type with roller bearing on drive side**

Right **Line drawing showing basic moving parts of W engine with valve gear exactly as BSA**

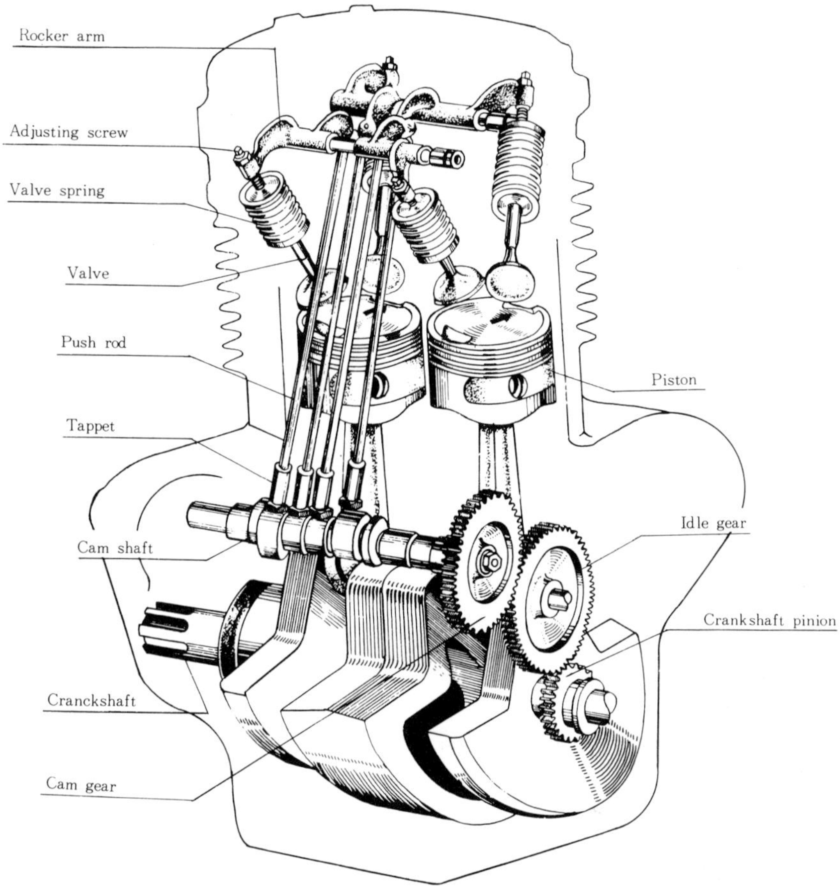

clamped up by five springs and lifted by a large diameter mushroom moved by a cable operated lever on the right whose assembly incorporated an adjusting screw.

The gearbox was English in design and mounted separately from the engine so pivoted to give primary chain tension adjustment. It contained four speeds which were selected by a positive stop mechanism controlled by a foot pedal on the right while the kick starter pedal was mounted on the same side. Both clutch and final drive sprockets went on the left and were concentric to one another while both gearbox shafts turned in ball races, the layshaft beneath the main.

Gear selection was by sliding one gear on each shaft in turn and thus top gear gave direct drive. The two selectors were positioned on a barrel cam mounted ahead of the two shafts and each carried a pin to run in the cam-track. The cam was controlled by a selector mechanism at the right end which coupled to the foot pedal. The kickstarter shaft carried a quadrant gear which meshed with a pinion on the mainshaft and a ratchet allowed this mechanism to turn the engine when the gearbox was in neutral. The layshaft carried a skew gear on its end and this meshed with a pinion below it which drove the speedometer cable. This instrument was matched by a rev-counter driven from the left

The W2TT Commander of 1969 with both high level exhaust systems on the left side, one above the other. Speedometer was not fitted into headlamp shell

end of the camshaft by a cable that ran up behind that corner of the barrel.

The engine and gearbox were held in place by plates and a head steady in a full cradle frame with pivoted fork rear suspension. At the front went telescopic forks with gaiters to protect the tubes and a straight-line steering damper to aid the handling and supplement the friction one also fitted.

Spoke wheels were used, both with full width hubs and 18 in. rims. The front tyre was of 3·25 in. section while the rear was a little fatter at 3·50 in. The front brake had two leading shoes, each with its own cam and pivot, and was 200 mm in diameter with 35 mm wide shoes. At the rear the diameter was reduced to 180 mm and the single leading shoe design used. A knockout spindle was used at the rear and the coupling between hub and sprocket incorporated a second shock absorber.

Sports section, stainless steel mudguards were fitted with the front supported by two stays on each side and the rear by a loop. The oil tank was matched by a side panel which hid the electrics and above these items went the dualseat. The fuel tank was fixed in place by a single central bolt hidden by a rubber plug just like a BSA and it held 15 litres. Chrome plated panels decorated each side and carried kneegrips and plastic badges.

The headlamps shell was fixed to the fork shrouds and was formed to carry the instruments in its top surface, this being raised to give the clearance needed. Both speedometer and rev-counter went under the same glass to give a combined unit and the housing also carried the warning lights for dynamo, neutral and main beam. Turn indicators were an optional fitting with the main section of their wiring included in the standard harness.

All told it made a handsome A10 replica and came in a choice of three colours for the tank, headlamp shell and side covers. It was the first big twin built by Kawasaki and quickly became the top selling large capacity model in Japan to account for 10 per cent of all the firm's sales. This was a quite remarkable figure in view of the small size of the over-250 cc market in Japan. It became the machine to own in its home country if you were into motorcycles and in addition the police force loved them. At the time it was Japan's largest and as happens so often the customers went for cubes.

Encouraged by this good response, Kawasaki

moved to establish themselves properly in the USA. In 1966 the Kawasaki Jidosha Hanbai Company changed its name to Kawasaki Motorcycles and American Kawasaki Motorcycle Corporation was set up in Chicago as a parts supply firm. A massive warehouse was built at Akashi, knockdown production began in Taiwan carried out by the Yuen Foong Industry company and a branch office was opened at Gardena. This was a suburb of Los Angeles and began the sale of motorcycles in California.

The W1 was a disaster in the USA. At home it may have been the greatest but abroad it had to meet the competition head on. It gave away a little capacity to the British 650 twins but that alone did not make the difference. It had to share the sales floor with the BSA A10 Rocket it copied and the word ran round America in no time flat. The Kawasaki could not cut it with the Spitfire, Bonneville, Constellation or Dominator and from that moment on it was a dead duck in the USA.

Once again Kawasaki had learnt that selling a machine built for and liked by the Japanese market was no guarantee that it would be successful abroad. In fact, the contrary seemed to apply, and once again Kawasaki thought about the American market and what it wanted.

Power, speed and acceleration was the answer and that is what they got with a taste in 1966 with a 250 cc twin cylinder 2-stroke, an appetiser in 1967 with a 350 cc version and a full meal late in 1968 with the advent of the 500 cc triple, the first of the superbikes. Later came the big four to consolidate the position but long before that the name Kawasaki was irrevocably linked with performance in capital letters.

Before that occurred, the company's position in the USA was consolidated by a number of moves. The first came early in 1967 when the Eastern Kawasaki Motorcycle Corporation was established in New Jersey and later that year when the American Kawasaki head office was moved from Chicago to Gardena.

That same year saw the first exports to the European market and some involvement with the classic racing scene but at a rather low level compared with the efforts made by Honda, Suzuki and Yamaha to secure titles from the Europeans in general and MV Agusta in particular.

It also brought some variations of the big twin W series. The first new model was the W2SS introduced in April 1967 as a street scrambler with more power gained from a modest rise in compression ratio to 9·0:1 and twin carburettors. The overall gearing was lowered by altering both gearbox and rear wheel sprockets and the silencers were changed for short tubular ones styled much as English types.

The mudguards were shortened and the stays changed so that the rear one became a grab handle. The seat was much thinner with a ribbed top surface and a small tail in the style known as tuck-and-roll in the USA. The bars were a little lower and laid back further so that hanging on at the claimed 115 mph must have been hard work. The front tyre diameter was increased to 19 in. and the rear section to 4·00 in., both tyres having block pattern treads.

Other claims included 87 miles to the US gallon at 31 mph which equalled 104 mpg on the English scale and a standing start quarter mile time of 13·7 seconds. Late in 1967 it was joined by the W1SS which was a street scrambler version of the W1 fitted with twin carburettors but none of these models were able to capture the imagination of the American buyers, although they had the cubic capacity asked for.

Kawasaki soldiered on with the big twin for a while but never with much heart and the advent of their lightweight, high performance, 2-stroke multis showed them the way they had to go. The W series was an anachronism from the days of the Meguro and only lived on like a dinosaur from the past in certain markets.

1968 brought the W1S model which was an improved version of the W1 and later a pair of police models. One was the W2P marketed in Australia and based on the W2 fitted out to police specification while the other was the W1SP based on the improved W1. That year also saw the first Kawasaki test course completed at Akashi.

In the middle of the year the W2TT model was announced as a touring version of the twin and its most noticeable feature was the exhaust system. Both pipes ran into one silencer mounted high on the left with twin outlets. The pipe from the left cylinder curled down to run along the top of the primary chaincase while that from the right curled across and under the left port to then run above the left pipe. In other respects it was as the W2SS and was known as the Commander.

At the end of 1968 the W1 was dropped and the W2TT went in 1969 along with the 250 cc singles, the SG and SGT. The W2SS ran to 1970 and the W1SS to 1971 but without any real interest from the market as the company had moved to much more exciting models which were taking all the attention.

In fact just about everyone outside the factory had forgotten the W series when in 1972 it appeared once more on the Japanese home market where it was sold as the 650-RS although the factory typing was W3. It was a domestic version of the W2 and filled a gap in the range until 1975 when it was replaced by a 750 cc twin and a 650 cc four. By that time it was showing its age badly but it had done a good job for the firm in its earlier years at home even if it had failed abroad.

Before the W series reached its end, the early Kawasaki 4-strokes were joined by one final model, the MB1 or Coyote. This must rate as the oddest Kawasaki of all and it was built for the North American and South Pacific markets.

It was a real primitive for the power unit was a single cylinder engine with side valves and no doubt came from the generator and stationary motor group. Dimensions were 60 × 47 mm, capacity 133 cc, compression ratio 6·4:1 and power output 3·4 bhp at 4200 rpm. It had a recoil pull handle starter, relied on splash lubrication, was fan cooled and had magneto ignition but no lights.

The engine drove a counter-shaft via an automatic centrifugal clutch and the two stage transmission was by chain and provided a single fixed gear. This limited the performance to a claimed 20 mph but would have been adequate for the short trips the model was built for.

The frame was a duplex cradle that ran back from the headstock, down to the rear wheel brackets, forward and up. The engine and countershaft sat on the lower rails and the small fuel tank and seat on the upper ones. Crude telescopics went onto the front with exposed springs and disc wheels were used fitted with 3·25 × 8 in. tyres with a block pattern. Mudguards were brief and only a rear brake was fitted so the controls were minimal with one for go and one for stop, both on the high rising handlebars.

All told a typical mini-bike and one of a breed that flourished in the sixties as an adjunct to car, boat or even plane to save shoe leather at minimal cost. In later years such duties were taken over by more sophisticated machines built as true motorcycles and for Kawasaki this led to the MT1 series of Mini Trail models. Purpose built, these were far more suited to their tasks than such devices as the Coyote so this faded from the range in 1971.

5 Twin cycles

The first Samurai model, the A1 of 1967, with twin cylinders, disc valves and plenty of go

During 1966 Kawasaki discovered that their big twin was not the answer they had hoped for in the large USA export market. It lacked excitement and, when offered alongside the traditional English twins, proved to be down in performance and style. Something else was needed with more panache and impact to suit the American market with its own special needs and foibles.

Acceleration seemed to be the key factor rather than pure speed, although that also was important. For the bulk of the large capacity machine buyers such things as economy, the ability to cruise at speed for long periods and the subtleties of handling and suspension were far outweighed by winning the stop-light grand prix. Such on-the-road contests were quick and easy and did not require the skills of a road racer in the turns. They were also exciting, and Kawasaki realized that this was the market they had to make an impact on if they wished to succeed.

Fortunately they had an alternative route to try to the blind alley they had been up. Instead of a large capacity, heavy machine with a passable power output, they could try something smaller, much, much lighter but still with adequate power. This was the path they chose and it took more than one step to achieve the front rank result they needed.

The first step was really a case of holding the fort on a temporary basis while they worked on the alternatives that were to make them king of the streets by two very different ways. This in-

Above **Brochure for the 350 cc version of the twin, the 1967 Avenger model A7. Different silencers but otherwise as the 250**

Right **The A7 as built for 1967–68 with twin leading shoe front brake and instruments in the headlamp shell**

terim measure was the A series of two-stroke twins and the first to be seen was the 250 cc A1 marketed as the Samurai and launched in May 1966. It was to become the first Kawasaki to sell well in the USA and it played a big part in establishing the company name around the world with a performance image.

The A1 was unusual for a road twin in that it had disc inlet valves and thus side-mounted carburettors with the attendant problems of width, inlet trunking and primary drive. Despite these it contrived to have line and style as the dimensions across the engine were kept down by mounting the generator behind the cylinders rather than on the crankshaft end. Thus both sides of the engine unit looked very similar as each had its carburettor hidden behind an alloy case but attended by a pair of control cables.

The engine was based on dimensions of 53 × 56 mm which gave a capacity of 247 cc and it conformed to normal two-stroke standards of build. The crankshaft had the pins at 180 degrees and ran on four ball main bearings with an oil seal between the two centre ones and one at each crankshaft end. The assembly was pressed together with full circle flywheels and the rims

of the outer wheels were chamfered to assist gas flow through the disc valve controlled inlet tract into the crankcase and up under the piston crown.

The two outer flywheels were forged with integral mainshafts, while the right inner wheel was similar and its shaft extended to the left inner wheel to which it was keyed. Balance was achieved using metal plugs pressed into holes in the flywheel sides. The assembly was positioned by the main bearings, one of which was located by a circlip to a groove in a bearing housing, these being provided for all the mains and located to the crankcase.

The connecting rods had needle races at both ends and the pistons were slightly offset and ran on circlip retained gudgeon pins. Two rings were fitted to each piston, both rectangular section but the top one was chrome plated while the second was chemically treated and had an expander ring installed behind it. The pistons had slightly domed crowns and gave a compression ratio of 7·0:1 actual.

Each one ran in a cylinder with a cast iron sleeve fused into an aluminium alloy muff with fins which were joined by vertical ribs to reduce ringing. The sleeve extended down to act as a spigot into the crankcase with cut-outs on each side to allow the gases to flow easily into the transfer passages. Each of these led to two ports in the cylinder, a main one set above the passage and a secondary one more to the rear to assist efficient scavenging. A single exhaust port was located at the front and the pipe was held by a collar which screwed on to the threaded port stub.

The barrels were topped by a pair of light alloy cylinder heads with central sparking plugs and the heads were well cooled with fins running from front to rear.

The lower half of the engine was built in unit with the five-speed gearbox, and the crankcase was split horizontally on the centre line of the crankshaft and the two gearbox shafts. The two case halves were machined to take the crankshaft at the front with two separate crank chambers and were finned externally to some extent. On each side was a disc valve chamber and each disc was cut from a 5 mm thick heat hardened, phenol resin sheet and attached to a cast steel centre keyed to the crankshaft.

An outer door enclosed the disc valve and carried the outer crankshaft seal. Cast into it was a stub for the carburettor so that this item could be clipped into position, and the outboard end of the crankshaft was used as a drive at each end. On the left went the oil pump and on the right the primary drive with both sides enclosed by a cover which carried further access plates. On the right these formed the outer part of the air trunking and gave access to the clutch adjust-

Above **The street scrambler version for 1967–68, the A1SS, with raised cross-over exhausts, braced bars and sump plate**

Right **The 250 cc A1SS looks unfinished without any exhaust on the right. Unsprung front guard made it more street than scrambler**

Left side of the 1967 Avenger A7. Ignition unit and generator were built into one assembly behind cylinder and cover is part of air trunking

ment, while on the left it again formed the air intake passage and boxed in the oil pump and its pipes.

The carburettors were of the conventional slide type with integral float chambers with twin floats either side of the main jet. They were supplied from the fuel tank via a three-position tap which gave a small reserve and had a filter built in. On the exhaust side the pipes were short and ran round to low set silencers on each side of the machine that began at the crankshaft and ran nearly to the back of the rear tyre.

The lubrication system used a pump to supply oil to the engine and the output from this varied according to the throttle opening as well as engine speed. The pump was mounted on the left disc valve cover and driven from the crankshaft by a gear pair. It was fed with oil from a tank mounted on the right side of the machine just below the seat and supplied oil via two pipes to each inlet tract. Each disc valve cover was machined for this and carried a check valve to prevent the oil flowing in the wrong direction and also to stop the flow as soon as the engine ceased to run. Upstream of this valve a nozzle carried the oil into the mixture stream in the tract and the resulting mist lubricated the engine. The throttle was linked to the oil pump by an extra cable which connected to a lever on the pump body and the two had to be set to synchronize to ensure a correct oil supply at all times.

The generator fitted to the first A1 was a permanent magnet alternator and the complete unit was mounted on top of the crankcase be-

Above **A1 engine with left side cover removed to show carburettor and engine oil pump linked to throttles; note also twin sets of points**

Left **Peter Chapman with an early A1R, the very fast road racing version of the 250**

hind the barrels under a cover. This cover also carried the air cleaner and acted as part of the air trunking to the carburettors. Drive to the generator was via the gear primary drive with a pinion on the end of the armature shaft meshing with the clutch drum. The three gear wheels were all marked for correct mesh alignment as the ignition cam and points were housed in the end of the generator remote from the drive. Coil ignition was employed and the generator ran at half engine speed so the ignition cam had twin lobes to open each pair of points the needed number of times. To assist correct timing one pair could be moved on the backplate which itself could be turned to adjust the other.

The primary drive was by helical gears directly to the clutch which was of conventional multi-plate design. It had five friction plates, four steel ones and six compression springs and the clutch was lifted by a ball and ramp mechanism set in the right engine cover. This pushed the clutch pressure plate to release the plates and allow the centre to run free.

The gearbox was an all-indirect, five-speed, cross-over design with the clutch on the right end of the front shaft and the output sprocket on the left end of the rear one. Three selector forks moved the appropriate gears to give the five ratios and each shaft was supported by one ballrace and one needle roller bearing. The selectors sat on a gear change drum and each had a guide pin which ran in a cam track cut in the drum. The drum end carried a row of pins and these were indexed round one at a time by the positive stop mechanism which terminated in a foot pedal on the left. As was normal Japanese practice, the pedal shaft extended across the crankcase and the change mechanism was all fitted on the right side behind the clutch.

The kickstart pedal folded and went on the right side of the machine. It had its own shaft and this carried a return spring and a gear to mesh with one on the gearbox output to transmit the rider's efforts to the crankshaft. Due to this system the machine had to be in neutral before the engine was started.

The final drive was by chain on the left with the gearbox sprocket held to the output shaft by a large nut against a spacer which ran in an oil seal to keep the lubricant internal. The rear wheel sprocket had lightening holes and the chain was protected by a small guard over the top run.

The engine and gearbox unit was installed in a full cradle frame with twin loops running from the headstock down under the unit and up to the rear end of the single top tube. This ran to the top of the headstock and was braced by a second tube beneath it, while the whole steering head area was stiffened by substantial pressings. Cross tubes beneath and behind the engine unit located the two frame loops and a cross-braced sub-frame was welded to them. This supported the rear suspension units and the seat while sub-loops on each side carried the pillion footrests and held up the silencers. A centre stand was fitted below the engine and a prop stand pivoted from a lug welded to the left frame loop while their use was assisted by a lifting handle bolted to the left side of the sub-frame at the top.

Rear suspension was by a pivoted fork controlled by a pair of spring units with hydraulic damping. At the front went telescopic forks, again with hydraulic damping, and the steering was assisted by a friction damper fitted under the lower crown and tightened by a knob at the top. The fork springs were external and fitted between the lower crown and the oil seal holder at the top of the leg with a gaiter over each spring to keep the dirt at bay.

Both wheels were built up with steel rims and wire spokes on a full width, light alloy, hub. Each contained a drum brake and at the front this had twin leading shoes with the two brake cams being linked externally by an adjustable rod, each shoe having its own pivot pin. At the rear a single leading shoe brake was used and a knockout spindle allowed the hub to be withdrawn leaving the rear wheel sprocket in place. A shock absorber went between the two to damp the drive line and the brake backplate was restrained by a torque arm. The brake was operated by a pedal on the right which coupled to a cable which ran back in a clean sweep to a cable stop on the backplate. In this way adjust-

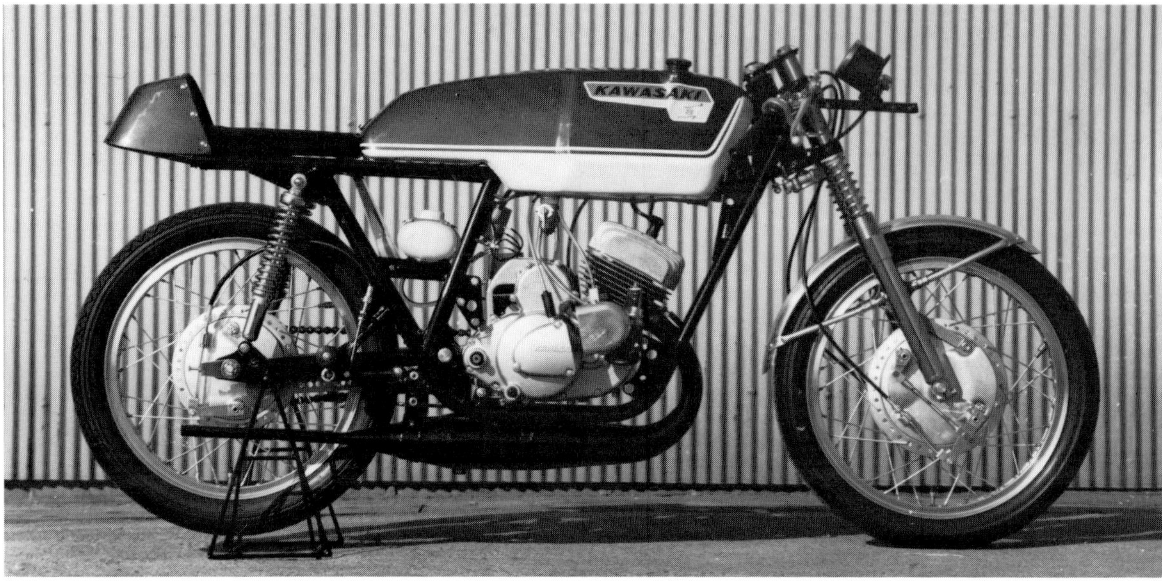

ment of the rear chain had no effect on that of the rear brake.

At the front the hub also contained the drive gear for the speedometer mounted in an upward extension of the headlamp shell and this instrument was mounted with the rev-counter beside it in the same housing under one transparent cover. Both moved in a clockwise direction and the rev-counter was driven from the oil pump drive.

Both wheels had 18 in. rims with a 3·00 in. tyre on the front and a 3·25 in. on the rear. The front mudguard was of the sports type in stainless steel and wrapped close to the tyre with a slim straight stay on each side to supplement the centre fixing. At the rear went a well valanced guard, and that one was chrome plated.

A dualseat was supplied and bolted to the frame. It had a two-tone covering, with black top and white sides, and was fitted with a seat strap. The fuel tank was painted in a contrasting two-tone finish and fitted with kneegrips and small plastic badges. The oil tank on the right carried a logo to remind the rider of the company name for their oil system, Superlube, and was matched by a cover on the left.

Some of the electrics lived behind this panel along with the battery, and the controlling switches were grouped on the handlebars with the ignition switch under the tank nose. Also on the bars was a lever which connected to the starter circuit of the carburettor to control the rich mixture needed when the engine was cold. Full lighting equipment was fitted including turn signals and stop light. The last was operated by a rear brake switch as standard but the option of a front switch was also offered. Warning lights for neutral and high main beam were provided.

Finish was in candy red or blue for the major part of the tank, the headlight shell, fork lamp brackets and rear unit top covers, with the lower part of the tank in white and the side cover and oil tank in silver. The frame was black but the bright colours and plentiful chrome plating made for a striking appearance, which was matched by the performance.

The power output was 31 bhp at 8000 rpm and rose in a straight line from 5 to 30 bhp so the torque curve was peaky with the maximum figure developed at 7500 rpm. Fortunately the

Far left **The 250 cc A1R showing the small shield fixed to each carburettor, small oil tank under seat and double front brake**

Left **The A1R with its correct fairing and stand as listed in the parts catalogue**

Below **Left side of A1R. Left cover was omitted and separate float chamber hung ahead of mixing one. Very remote gearchange and long tailpipes**

output at 6000 rpm was nearly as high and this made the power band adequately wide.

The dry weight was 319 lb so it was no surprise that Kawasaki claimed a standing quarter time of 15 sec. while maximum speed was quoted as 103 mph. This was perhaps a touch optimistic as on the standard gearing the engine would have been turning over at around 9000 rpm at that speed, or a thousand revs above the normal maximum. The Kawasaki power graph indicates that by then power had fallen to around 22 bhp and thus re-gearing and a small rider would have been needed to reach the magic ton.

The factory data also suggested 100 mpg, and US gallons at that, at 30 mph but while this may have been possible the likelihood of it ever occurring was highly remote. The claimed braking figure of 39 ft for a stop from 31 mph seemed rather poor for the machine weight and brake specification but might have been improved by a change in lining material.

What the A1 did do really well was accelerate from a standstill and in no time at all they were seen about California upsetting owners of much larger machines at the stop light grand prix. In a very short space of time Kawasaki had the image they were seeking and their name quickly became associated with performance.

At the end of 1965 they introduced a special variant typed the A1R and built solely for road racing. It was based on the road machine but with a good many modifications to both engine and chassis. Internally the port timing was altered and the compression ratio raised to 8·0:1, this being the actual ratio taken from the point of exhaust port closure.

Right **Dave Simmonds on the 350 cc A7R in 1968**

Far right **Kent Andersson on the 250 at Scarborough in 1967**

The standard carburettors went and were replaced by a pair of 26 mm racing Mikuni mixing chambers with remote floats mounted forward of them. In this position they tended to richen the mixture when accelerating and on gradients, while weakening it for the reverse, that is braking and descents, all of which helped the performance and reduced the chance of plug oiling. Each carburettor had a small shield around the bellmouth to prevent turbulence disturbing the air flow, and naturally the air cleaner was dispensed with along with the associated trunking.

On the exhaust side went expansion boxes held to the cylinders with springs and to the frame by flexible brackets. The boxes were of a fairly small volume and fitted with long, small diameter tailpipes. Ignition was by magneto with external coil and the throttle controlled oil pump was retained. It was supplied from a small tank strapped to the battery tray of the frame beneath the seat and the contents were supplemented by running the engine on a petroil mixture of 15:1 ratio.

The left engine cover was dispensed with completely as was the front part of the right but the rear had to remain as it carried the clutch release mechanism. The result of all the work was 40 bhp at 9500 rpm and a top speed of 125 mph, certainly competitive for the era.

To handle the extra power the primary drive gears were changed to the spur form and the ratio altered. The overall gearing was raised and the gearbox fitted with a close ratio set. The kickstarter shaft remained and could be used if a pedal was fitted but normally the machine was bump started in traditional racing style.

On the chassis side the same basic frame layout was retained along with similar rear units and front forks minus gaiters but with a small amount of extra movement. Both hubs were changed to ones containing larger brakes and at the front went a double sided light alloy drum with twin leading shoes on each side. The size rose from the 180 mm diameter and 30 mm width of the road model to 200 × 20 mm each side. Restraint of each backplate was by a torque arm and the two cam levers were connected by an adjustable rod with one lever extended for its cable. Both cables ran up to the handlebar lever. The rear brake increased its width only to 180 × 36 mm and the hub remained a full width, light alloy type with the sprocket on the left but without the knockout spindle. The torque arm was amended to be fully floating, while operation remained by a sweeping cable, this time with the adjuster screwed into the backplate lug.

Wheel rims were light alloy and racing covers were fitted, still of 18 in. diameter but with slightly reduced sections at 2·75 and 3·00 in. No rear mudguard was fitted as the racing seat had a short tail to deal with this function and the front one was short, close fitting, and braced with a straight stay on each side. The fuel tank was longer and larger than that of the road model

Right below **A7R engine minus barrels and one piston so transfer passage at rear of crankcase can be seen**

Below **Same machine showing its road model origins quite clearly. An adaptation that worked very well**

with a fuel tap with filter on each side to supply each carburettor.

The footrests used the pillion rest lugs to support them with the brake pedal on the right and the gearchange on the left connected to the box by a long rod. Clip-ons were fitted to the forks just below the top crown and the headstock had a fairing bracket attached to it which carried the mechanically driven rev-counter. A neat fairing with bulges for the carburettors was normally fitted.

In the traditions of the American market the A1 and the racing model were followed up in February 1967 in the vein of 'give them the same but make it bigger and brighter'. The result was the A7, with more capacity, and the A1SS, a street scrambler version of the road 250, built for and only sold in North America.

At first sight the A7 was just the 250 with the bore opened up to 62 mm to increase the capacity to 338 cc. This was emphasised by the compression ratio which remained unaltered and the port timings which only changed by a degree or two. In fact there were other more subtle modifications to improve the oiling system and the ability of the drive line to take the rise in power.

Aside from the extra capacity the power increase came as much as anything from the larger 28 mm carburettor size. No subtle move but it did push the power up to 42 bhp at 8000 rpm. To cater for this the lubrication of the bottom half was modified to supply oil to the big ends and the new system called 'Injectolube'.

In this the crankshaft driven oil pump was retained along with the throttle control but the output was increased by 20 per cent to cope with the higher loads and extra deliveries called for. As on the A1, oil was pumped into the inlet tract but in addition it was fed to the outer side of the outside main bearing. It flowed through this and was collected by a disc screwed to the flywheel and flared to touch the main to capture the oil and rolled in at its periphery to prevent its easy escape. The only avenue left open for it was a hole drilled partway through the crankpin to a cross hole which fed the big end needles.

The transmission kept the same primary gears but had one more pair of plates fitted into the clutch and clamped up by different springs. To allow the plates to fit they were thinner than on the 250. The overall gearing was raised by reducing the size of the rear wheel sprocket by one tooth. The wheels were of the same diameter and with the same brakes and hubs but the front rim section was increased to match that at the rear and the tyre sections went up to 3·25 in. front and 3·50 in. rear.

Externally the larger machine had a number of features to distinguish it from the A1. The seat was one for it had a ribbed top and was in black with just white piping as a contrast. The fuel tank had chrome plated side panels which carried

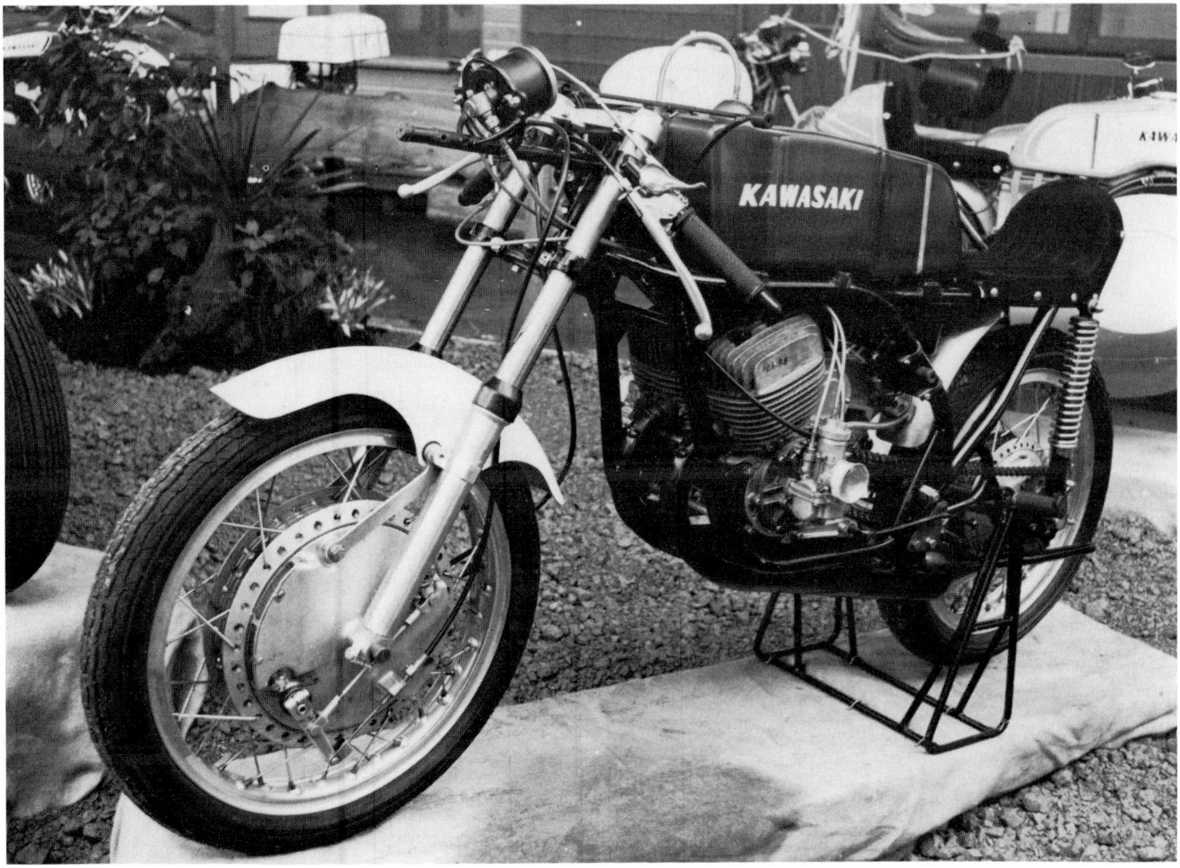

both the kneegrips and the badges, while the silencers were different and had stub tailpipes of large diameter.

To assist the handling a linear hydraulic steering damper was fitted but the friction one complete with its adjusting knob was retained. Finally, on the side cover went a new label with the model's name 'Avenger' and '350 injectolube', to reinforce the message to A1 and owners of other two-stroke twins that this was a big one and not to be trifled with.

There was no doubt it went and the claimed standing quarter time was 13·8 seconds. Top speed was given as 110 mph and again this would have meant running the engine way past the peak speed to around 9500 rpm if it had been

Above **A1RA, the final version of the racing 250 with float chambers integral with carburettors**

Right above **Drive side of A1RA showing carburettor and dry clutch very clearly, also spring retained exhausts and maybe compression ratios, geometric and actual, penned on cylinder head**

kept on standard gearing. Consumption was reduced from that of the 250 but only to 80 to the US gallon. Again no-one ever rode an Avenger at 30 mph to see if it would record this figure, and such was the exhilarating performance that 30 mpg at 80 mph was by far the more normal mark, and that on Imperial gallons as well.

The second new model, the A1SS, was a street scrambler for the US market. It was much as the A1 with mainly cosmetic changes and used the stock 250 engine and gearbox unit. The gearing was lowered by a rear sprocket with two more teeth and the brakes remained as on the A1. The front tyre kept to the A1 section but changed to a block tread type, while the rear one was increased to 3·50 in.

The most striking feature of the machine was the twin exhausts both of which ran high up on the left side. The pipes crossed over in front of the cylinders so that the one from the right ran above the left port but then curved closely round the engine to the silencer. The left pipe came more forward before turning up and round the right to finish above it and connect to the upper silencer. Both silencers terminated in tailpipes with end caps and both were fitted with perforated heat shields along their length to protect rider and passenger.

Because of the exhaust system run no left side cover was fitted and to allow access to the space behind it, the seat was hinged on one side. The seat itself had more of a tail than on the A1 and was in black with contoured white piping.

It made a stylish model and the lower gearing made the acceleration better, although the claimed top speed must have been even further out of reach than on the A1. For its market this was none too important as it was acceleration that pulled in the customers.

KAWASAKI

In October 1967 Kawasaki did the obvious and produced a street scrambler version of the larger twin and called it the A7SS. It mirrored the changes that had turned the A1 into the A1SS but retained the chrome tank panels of the A7 plus braced handlebars and a skid plate. The exhausts were as on the smaller model, although on occasion either had minor changes to the tail-pipe to meet the spark arrester requirements.

Left **The A1A model, the 1970 version of the 250 cc twin with separate instruments, new marking and slimmer rear mudguard**

Below **1971 A1B with another change to the colour and marking but otherwise little altered**

They all stayed unchanged during 1968 and continued to build up the Kawasaki name for exciting motorcycling. Late in the year they were eclipsed by the advent of the first triple and the struggle to lead the power stakes moved up a gear to leave the twins behind. While they became overshadowed both by their own stable-mate and also by the new big Honda, they continued to be desirable and filled in the middle range for Kawasaki for several more years.

The A1R was only built for two seasons and was joined by the A7R for a while. This followed the same format to make a larger capacity model and was bored out one more millimetre to 63 mm and a full 349 cc. It ran on a 7·7:1 compression ratio, more radical timing and breathed through 29 mm carburettors to produce 53 bhp at 9500 rpm. Claimed top speed was 138 mph

and it used the same chassis as the A1R right down to the tyres.

In 1969 there were mainly styling changes to the road models and the only technical modification was the adoption of capacitor discharge ignition on both the SS models and the A1 and A7 when sold in the USA. Thus this effectively meant electronic ignition for North America as the SS was not offered elsewhere.

The fuel tanks lost their kneegrips and were given a paint finish with the marque name in bold letters, while the headlamp shell lost the instruments. These were mounted separately from the top fork crown while the shell became smaller to just accommodate the light unit and the wiring. The seat of the standard models was changed to the same style as that of the SS and the rear units lost their spring covers again as on the street scramblers. Finally the line of the front mudguard stays was altered to introduce two small bends in them.

Above **Last in the 350 cc line, the 1971 model A7B, an exciting machine**

Right **The racing 350 cc twin, the A7R, with expansion boxes and double front brake**

The four twins were now set to run to the end of their production lives for interest had turned away from them and Kawasaki needed other models to sustain their power image. They had, however, helped the firm to establish themselves

outside Japan and this was reflected by a number of company events in 1969.

The first came in January when American Kawasaki and Eastern American combined to form Kawasaki Motors Corporation at Gardena. Two months later they relocated at Santa Ana, still in California, and then in April came a major regrouping in Japan. Kawasaki Aircraft Industries, Kawasaki Dockyard and Kawasaki Rolling Stock came together to form Kawasaki Heavy Industries, which then continued as the controlling company for all their many fields of activity.

A futher reason for their success in the USA was a policy of near complete autonomy for the Californian office which was staffed with Americans and left in peace to get on with their job of selling and supporting the make. Thus it was able to develop to suit its own market and followed its own needs, not those of the parent company.

1969 saw the larger twins also on offer under the American Eagle brand with the A7 sold as the Marauder and the street scrambler as the Cheetah. Both used the mechanics of the stock machine but were fitted with new tanks and a long seat base that ran back to the tail light, plus matching side panels.

Early in 1970 Kawasaki began knockdown production in the Philippines with the Delsa Industrial Corporation and in September that year established Kawasaki Motors NV, in Holland to act as a parts centre for Europe. The company had used a number of independent distributors around Europe in the late 1960s but, having

English magazine advert for the early Samurai placed by the then UK concessionaires and including the Kawasaki Aircraft, Tokyo origins and the race machine enquiries address

established themselves in America, now wished to begin the same process in the heart of the original centre of motorcycling. A few Kawasaki machines had reached the shores of England by that time and the marque had become known to enthusiasts in that country and others thanks to the efforts of Dave Simmonds on the race circuits with a 125 cc twin as well as those of 250 and 350 cc.

Around 1967 the UK concessionaires were C. Itoh in London and the parent factory was still given as Kawasaki Aircraft of Tokyo. They exhibited at Earls Court that year and sold the A7 off the stand, although at that time no engine spares were in the country. It was a rare machine in England then but made a great contrast to the usual vertical twins. At the same time a few racing models reached the country and they were handled by Peter Chapman, thanks to a visit he had made to Japan for their grand prix.

This was all very hand to mouth and untidy so was superseded by a concession agreement with Agrati sales who were already in business importing and selling one or two European scooter and moped ranges. Thanks to this they had a feel for the market and the needed trade contacts so were able to build up a small dealer network but this arrangement only continued to the end of 1973.

The A series of models ran on into the 1970s but their position in their capacity classes was then taken over by the newer triples. Changes were therefore minimal and for 1970 all four models were treated alike and given an A suffix to the type. Changes were made to the fuel tank which became longer and lower to lose the earlier humped appearance, while the seat styling altered with the disappearance of the piping and the fitment of a thin plated bead along the seat base. The rear mudguard lost its valance and became more sporting and both colour and markings were altered.

1971 was the final year for all four when they were given a B suffix and colour and marking changes. The Two SS models also had the exhaust pipe finish changed to matt black with the heatshield to match.

It brought to an end a period during which Kawasaki progressed from a range of small singles and old Meguros to having a name for performance for a class. They now had to build on that for their performance absolute image.

Right **A page from a booklet issued by KHI, the booklet giving some of their motorcycle and company history since 1878. Details and pictures of new models go hand in hand with business expansion and some competition success**

1967

CORPORATE AFFAIRS:

Mar. • In order to intensify sales in the Eastern regions of North America, Kawasaki establishes a branch office in the state of New Jersey called Eastern Kawasaki Motorcycle Corp. (EKM).

• Kawasaki initiates exports to the European market.

Aug. • Kawasaki relocates the head office of American Kawasaki Motors Corp., from Chicago, Illinois to Gardena, California.

MOTORCYCLE PRODUCTION:

Feb. • **A7** (350cc, 2-str., 2-cyl., 5-speed)–incorporates the same frame as the A1, and is marketed as the "Avenger".

• **C1DL**–a C1L with an electric starter.

• **C2SS** (120cc, 2-str., 1-cyl., 4-speed)–marketed as the "Roadrunner".

• **A1SS**–an A1 with street scrambler specifications.

Mar. • **G1M**–a motocross version of the G1.

• **C2TR**–a dual purpose version of the C2SS, marketed as the "Roadrunner".

Apr. • **W2SS** (650cc, 4-str., 2-cyl., 4-speed)–an improved version of the W1 with a street scrambler specifications.

June • **M50** (50cc, 2-str., 1-cyl., 3-speed)

• **G1DL**–a G1L with an electric starter.

Oct. • **A7SS**–a street scrambler version of the A7, marketed as the "Avenger".

Dec. • **W1SS**–a street scrambler version of the W1 with twin carburetors.

A7 "AVENGER"

A1SS "SAMURAI"

RACE RESULTS:

MFJ ALL-JAPAN CHAMPIONSHIP MOTOCROSS SERIES

FINAL STANDINGS

90cc	T. Yamamoto	1st
250cc	T. Yamamoto	1st
"	K. Hoshino	2nd

C2SS

G1M

W2SS

M50

6 Hot triples

The early Mach III or 500-SS, 'the triple with the ripple' and the reputation for a real, exciting ride. 1969 model

The disc valve two-stroke twins that Kawasaki introduced in 1966 were very fast for their class and could often surprise owners of much larger machines but in the final analysis a good 650 was faster. However, the twins were just an interim measure and while they helped to establish the Kawasaki name for performance, the company worked on a new model that was to overshadow them.

This was to be a machine that was not only top in its class but was also able to outrun just about everything else on the road. It was the first real superbike and was to become a legend thanks to its performance, doubtful handling, considerable thirst and wild character.

Never a machine to take home to mother, it grabbed attention and fans as easily as it radiated excitement. It was the model H1 with a 500 cc, three cylinder engine set in line across the frame and was marketed in Japan as the '500-SS' and known to the rest of the world as the Mach III.

It made its debut in September 1968 and its light weight and exuberant power output were a sure guarantee of an exciting time for anyone who climbed aboard. Power to weight ratio ensured the startling acceleration but that power allied to a low all up weight meant a twitchy ride in a straight line even if the surface was super smooth.

In theory, the same result should come from a heavier machine with more power, but even if the ratio remains the same the ride changes.

The higher inertia alters the machine's reaction to road irregularities and always seems to bring a less lively ride. The Kawasaki chassis was in truth too light for the power and this just aggravated the trait.

The H1 was based on three cylinders set in line across the frame, piston controlled inlets and a 5-speed gearbox built in unit with the engine. The firing intervals were evenly spaced at 120 degrees so the engine output and torque were very smooth, but in balance a three has a rocking couple along its crankshaft so suffers from vibration. This added to the excitement it generated as it leapt from bump to bump and corner to corner with the front wheel as often as not clear of the ground.

The engine of the triple had dimensions of 60 × 58·8 mm so the capacity of each cylinder was 166 cc and the total was 499 cc. The heart of the engine was the lengthy crankshaft which was a pressed-up assembly and ran on a total of six main bearings. Four oil seals were fitted, two at the shaft ends and two between the inner pairs of mains, and the six small flywheels were a close fit in the crankcase and each pair ran close to the connecting rod with a machined recess for the big end. As on the twins, both ends of the rods contained needle bearings.

The gudgeon pin was offset by 0·5 mm towards the inlet side of the piston to reduce slap and was retained by two circlips. The piston was quite conventional with a domed crown giving an actual compression ratio of 6·8:1 and cut outs at the sides to aid gas flow. Two piston rings were fitted, the upper chrome plated, and the second groove also contained an expander ring.

The light alloy cylinder heads were well finned and had central sparking plugs. Each was held by 4 sleeve nuts on long studs screwed into the top of the crankcase and these also retained the barrels. The cylinders were inclined forward slightly and were cast in light alloy with cast iron sleeves around which the alloy was poured to get a really good, fused bond to give the best possible heat conduction.

Thanks to the wide spread of the cylinders all three were well finned, with the centre one having little less width than the two outers. Porting was straightforward with single rectangular inlet and oval exhaust. Both ports were wide with the exhaust 39 mm and the inlet 46 mm with a 4 mm central bridge.

Four transfer ports were provided with each pair supplied by a single passage. The main port was above this passage while the smaller secondary one was positioned more to the rear and had its sides angled to assist gas flow. Both ports had the same timing.

Each cylinder was fitted with an inlet tract held on a pair of studs and this carried a clip fitting slide carburettor of 28 mm bore. On the exhaust side a further pair of studs took the collar which clamped the exhaust pipe into place. The carburettors all breathed from a common air filter set

Right **The H1 from the left; looks like a twin but packs two gun barrels on the right**

Opposite above **The H1 frame, fully duplex and 'not dissimilar' to the Norton featherbed (in shape) with crossed tubes behind the headstock**

Opposite below **The H1R complete with Kawasaki fairing and battery hung from the frame to power ignition system**

Below **1969 Mach III prepared for production racing and invoking plenty of interest in the paddock. Some ripple**

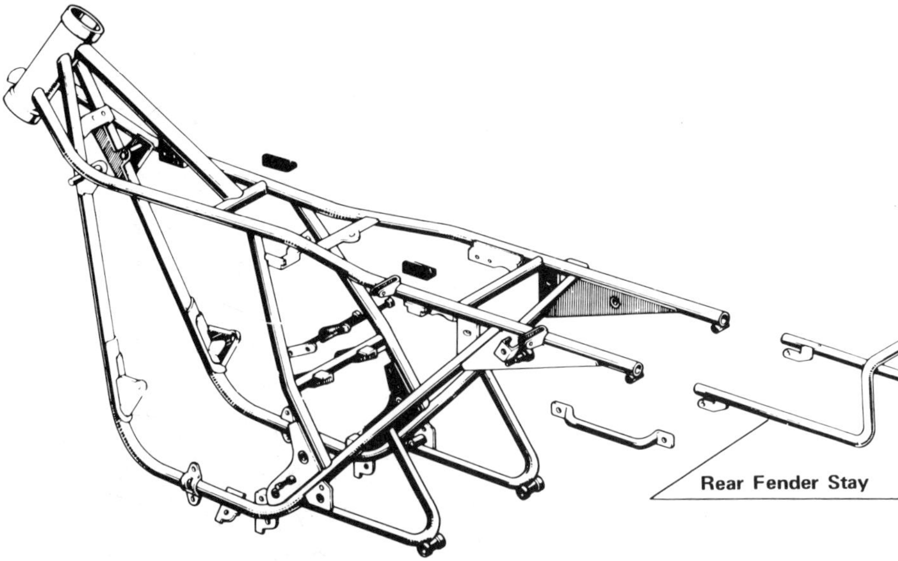
Rear Fender Stay

KAWASAKI
KAWASAKI

Right **The Kawasaki team at Ontario in 1971 with a works triple, mechanic Randy Hall on the right. Lovely big front drum brake**

Below **The 1971 H1A with a new tank in a different colour and markings, otherwise as original model**

vertically behind them and connected by a three legged hose so the intake was high up under the rear of the tank.

Unlike the intake, the exhausts remained separate to the ends of the silencers. Each cylinder had its own system and this comprised the short pipe clamped to the exhaust port by the collar and a long silencer with detachable baffle in its tail. With three cylinders the result was inevitably uneven and two pipes were run on the right and one on the left to give the machine its unique appearance. Of the pair of pipes the right cylinder fed to the higher silencer with the centre one running inboard of it to emerge low down and tucked into the rear wheel.

The bottom half of the engine was of typical modern two-stroke construction with the main crankcase split horizontally through the centre of the crankshaft and the gear shafts. The two parts were cast in light alloy and held in alignment by two pins. A considerable number of studs joined them together and were screwed into the top half with nuts on the underside and the lower case was well ribbed to improve rigidity.

The crankshaft sat with its flywheels in close fitting chambers and was positioned by the mains which were located by set rings. Close behind it went the gearbox input shaft with the clutch on the right and behind that the output shaft with the final drive sprocket on the left. Astern of that went the kickstarter shaft with its spindle protruding to the right to carry the pedal and the case was a close fit around the complete assembly.

Due to the width of the crankshaft, the left chamber hung out from the main box of the other two cylinders and the transmission, but by placing it ahead of the sprocket this effect was partially hidden. The width of the engine was made more by the fitment of electrics at both ends of the crankshaft and thanks to this it had to be mounted well up to give cornering clearance.

The ignition system was capacitor discharge and this was the first time such was fitted to a production road machine. It fired surface discharge sparking plugs and the extra high voltage reduced any tendency to plug oiling or overheating to a minimum. It was a battery powered circuit with the 12 volts direct source current having to be turned into alternating, transformed and then rectified back to direct but up at 400 volts. This charged the capacitor which was discharged into the primary circuit of the ignition coil by an electronic switch. This took the form of a thyristor and was triggered by a small signal generated by one of three permanent magnets turning close to a coil. The magnet assembly was mounted on the extreme left end of the crankshaft and the coil signal was sent via a screened cable to an amplifier and then to a trigger contained in one box.

The result was a potential of 30,000 volts from the ignition coil three times in every crankshaft revolution and this was dispatched to the correct plug by a distributor mounted on the extreme right and gear driven from the crankshaft. An outer cover enclosed the distributor cap and encouraged the leads to run behind the cylinders and up to the plugs.

It was an advanced system, and like most of its type, gave benefits and problems. It certainly reduced plug trouble and improved starting while there was in theory no maintenance as there were no parts to wear. In practice the system could develop its own quirks and faults, it could suffer false triggering with the mixture going off at any old time and ignition timing became a new science. Kawasaki provided markers on the magnet rotor and gave instructions on setting the piston position and aligning the marks. Less emphasized was the importance of getting the timing right, the absolute need to check it at 4000 rpm and no mention made of the good quality strobe needed to do this. Furthermore, with two boxes of electronics, a signal generator, ignition coil, supply lines and earths,

there were a good number of electrical connections in the circuit and few realized the potential for damage that the odd loose one could create.

Properly connected it worked well but any error, even connecting the battery wrongly, could stop it in its tracks and do expensive damage. It was fine for a competition machine but with the state of the art as it was in 1968, Kawasaki were well out on a limb. The position of the alternator just inboard of the signal generator was a further potential ignition trouble spot but in its own field the item worked well with a rectifier to convert the output to direct current for the battery and a regulator controlling the field current.

Lubrication of the engine was by the injectolube system with the oil pump mounted on top of the cover that bolted to the right side of the crankcase and concealed the primary transmission. Inside the cover a horizontal shaft ran across ahead and below the crankshaft with the distributor at its outer end and a plastic spur gear at the inner which meshed with one fixed to the crankshaft end. Above it were a pair of helical gears with the front larger plastic one driving the rev-counter and the rear one, in steel, the oil pump. Both gears were driven by a worm which meshed with the oil pump gear and this was secured to the end of the crankshaft by a single bolt.

The oil pump was of the variable output type with a control linked to the three throttle cables. Each cylinder had its own oil supply and as on the twins, this went via a check valve into the

Above **The 1972 S2 or Mach II, 350 cc from three cylinders and very fast and very thirsty. Twin leading shoe brake became a disc for 1973**

Left **Another view of the S2 showing the run of the twin silencers on the right. Quite one of the best looking motorcycles of the decade with novel tail fairing**

main bearings, and thence to the big end. A bleed was taken up into the inlet tract so that oil was fed into the mixture just as in the disc valve engine. Main bearings that did not receive the benefit of the pumped supply were lubricated by drains in the transfer passages in the upper crankcase.

The primary drive was by a single pair of straight cut gears on the right side of the engine unit. The crankshaft gear was positioned against the right main bearing for maximum support with the smaller distributor drive gear outboard of it. The clutch gear was riveted to the drum and ran on a needle race mounted on the gearbox input shaft. The clutch was conventional with 7 friction and 6 steel plates clamped together by 5 springs. The lifting mechanism was a cable pulled lever and quick thread on the left working a push rod and pressure plate mushroom through the gearbox shaft.

The gearbox was a 5 speed, all indirect, crossover type with fairly close ratios. The input shaft ran in a ball race behind the clutch and a needle race while the output had the same plus a further ball race close up to the output sprocket. Set rings located the ball races and a catch plate collected oil and fed it to the output shaft needle race.

The gears themselves ran directly on the shafts in the order 1, 5, 3, 4, 2 from the clutch side. Third gear on the input and fourth and fifth on the output slid to engage the gears with the first selecting the top two ratios, the second the next two and fifth on the output being responsible for first gear only. The three selector forks ran on the selector drum and this had the cam tracks cut into it so that guide pins located the forks to them. Pins in the end of the drum were indexed round one at a time by the positive stop mechanism. This was contained in the space behind the clutch with the operating shaft extending across the crankcase to the left side where it emerged low down. It appeared at a point below the output sprocket just outside the small cover that enclosed this and which was styled to mate with the one over the generator and ignition trigger. From this point the shaft was connected to the gear pedal by a short external linkage, the pedal being pivoted on the frame just behind the left footrest.

The covers were matched on the right by the primary drive one which carried the kickstarter shaft. The internal mechanism differed from the pawl and ratchet of the A series twins but the final result was to turn the crankshaft via the bottom gear on the output shaft so the machine had to be in neutral for starting. Neutral was below first gear and required a full movement of the pedal to select it, something some riders had problems in coping with.

The engine unit was thus a blend of well tried practice such as the wide ports and small flywheels coupled with the advanced CDI in a well engineered package. The result was 60 bhp at 7500 rpm and peak torque at 7000 rpm, while the already steep power curve that ran from 3000 to 6000 rpm increased its gradient as the output shot from 45 to 55 bhp in 500 revs. Over the years 6000 rpm was to remain the key point in the triple's performance and the place where the power took off.

The engine unit was installed in a frame which in retrospect proved to be carrying it too far to the rear. Dry and unladen, the rear wheel took 57 per cent of the weight, and this was to become a source of some embarrassment to riders in the years to come. The frame itself was a full duplex cradle with an added single headstock brace.

The top tubes ran from the bottom of the headstock back along the line of the tank and seat to a point behind the rear unit fixings. Into the tail ends of the tubes went a rear loop bent up behind the seat to form a grab handle. From the top of the headstock a single tube ran back to brace the top tubes and just below this went the two down tubes. These ran between the top pair to the front engine mounting, under the unit

1972 advert for the S2 placed by Agrati Sales who were the UK concessionaires at that time

and then up to the top tubes, this junction being well braced by gussets that carried the top rear unit studs. A pair of tubes ran up from the area of the rear fork pivot to the top tubes and various cross tubes held the two loops together. Extra, small loops carried the pillion footrests and supported the silencers, while a large gusset on each side took the rear fork pin.

The rear fork was of welded tubular construction and moved on bushes. It was restrained by a pair of hydraulically damped spring units with a three position preload available for the spring. At the front went telescopic forks, again with hydraulic damping of the movement, with internal springs and no gaiters. Their movement in the head bearings was restrained by a friction damper and there was an option of an in-line hydraulic one to supplement this for the USA market.

Both wheels were built onto full width, light alloy hubs but differed in other respects. The front hub contained a 200 mm diameter twin leading shoe drum brake 35 mm wide with a separate pivot pin and cam for each shoe. The cam levers were joined externally by an adjustable rod and the forward one extended for the operating cable. The hub was spoked into a steel rim and this carried a 3·25 × 19 in. tyre.

At the rear the hub contained a 180 mm diameter single leading shoe brake 35 mm wide and this was cable operated directly from the brake pedal on the right. The backplate was vented with inlet and outlet air holes and the plate extended down to a torque arm which ran to a point on the rear fork just aft of the pivot. The rear wheel spindle was of the knockout type so a separate sleeve supported the rear sprocket and allowed it to remain in situ while the wheel was removed. Between the two went a shock absorber and the hub was spoked to a smaller but wider rim carrying a 4·00 × 18 in. tyre.

The front mudguard was in stainless steel and close fitting with a single straight stay on each side. The rear one was also of sporting section and braced on the underside to maintain a clean line to the tail light and rear number plate. The

The 250 cc triple, the S1 or Mach I, very similar to the S2 and to run on for a good few years; popular with young riders of the day

dualseat was pivoted along the left edge and had a humped tail and a plated strip along each side. Pillion footrests were fitted as standard and like them, the main footrests could fold up, although to a lesser extent.

The fuel tank held 15 litres of petrol and this went to the three carburettors via an automatic fuel tap turned on by the suction of the engine intake. The tap assembly included a filter and its control lever gave normal, reserve and prime positions, the last allowing fuel to flow even if the engine was not running. The oil tank was mounted on the right side of the machine below the seat and had a capacity of 2·3 litres. At the rear end a plastic tube ran up the outside of the tank to provide a level gauge and a single pipe carried the oil to the pump.

On the other side of the machine went a matching cover and between it and the oil tank nestled the battery, some electrics and the tools. The electric circuits were controlled by an ignition switch and an assembly of knobs on the left handlebar. The ignition key gave a parking light facility and ignition on with or without lights. The bar console provided the horn button, dipswitch and the turn indicator control, these being an option which could be plugged into the existing wiring system. Separate switches worked by the front and rear brake controls turned on the stop light.

Controls were conventional with a choke lever built into the twistgrip housing connected to all three carburettors. Less usual were the gearchange and rear brake pedals which could be reversed using a Kawasaki kit of parts to put the gear lever on the right and the brake on the left in the English style.

Instruments were the rev-counter plus a front wheel driven speedometer mounted side by side at the top of the forks. Warning lights were provided for neutral, main beam and indicators when fitted, while when at rest the machine was held up by either a centre or prop stand.

That then was the Mach III and with 60 horses to propel a dry weight of 382 lb there was little doubt that it would be a flier. Kawasaki claimed 118 mph and a standing quarter in 12·4 seconds but failed to mention whether both were performed on the same gearing. Even with European sprockets the engine had to run close to

Right **The underside of the 1972 H1B showing the run of the three exhaust systems and the way the stands were formed to clear them**

Left **The 1972 H1B standing at the end of the long straight at Snetterton race circuit. First year with disc front brake**

9000 rpm for this speed and in the USA with a gearbox sprocket with one less tooth it was well over that figure. Both were far above the 7500 rpm quoted as the peak horsepower speed.

An early American test confirmed this with the top speed a staggering 124 mph using the larger gearbox sprocket and a quarter time of 13·2 seconds. At the start of 1969 this was an astonishing performance for any machine and quite incredible for a mere 500. At a stroke Kawasaki had confirmed their performance image and enhanced their reputation.

The acceleration of the Mach III coupled with the short wheelbase and light weight made for an exciting ride even when in a straight line. Sit normally on the seat and the front wheel would climb for the sky as the clutch went home. Sit forward and the special Dunlop K77 on the rear wheel would spin and smoke. On US gearing the effect was even more startling even if the top speed was a mite down. One journalist suggested that maybe the more impetuous riders would get into some difficulties with the model after he had ridden one a few miles. It was a classic of understatements.

Violent acceleration and abrupt wheelies were exciting but not too hard to learn to control, but the triple did not leave it at that. The power band had its abrupt kink around 6000 rpm when it was already churning out enough power to see off nearly every other machine on the road. At that point more horses joined in with a will to jolt any feeling of security, and further strain the rear tyre to break its grip of the tarmac.

This sudden power surge could and did make cornering interesting. Banging the throttle open

at the wrong point would pick the front wheel off the deck with complete disregard to the rider's feelings and put it down again well out of line with the rear one. Minor gurgles in the carburettors could have enlivening effects quite out of proportion to their size and riders very soon learnt the true meaning of smooth throttle control.

Then there was the frame to add to the already frantic package and this combination did more than stir the adrenalin, it brought it to the boil. The frame was quite nice as far as it went but this was just not far enough. It copied, to a degree, the famous Norton featherbed with cross-over tubes just behind the headstock but lacked

Above **That H1B on test with** *Motorcycle Mechanics* **in 1972, then editor Charles Deane in the saddle**

Right **The big one, the 750 cc triple H2 or Mach IV as launched in 1972 with single disc front brake**

some of the complete rigidity of the English version, and even that was known to object to an excess of power and give problems if asked to cope with too much.

The Kawasaki frame was just not up to the task of harnessing 60 busy horses and so it flexed and weaved especially on bumpy corners taken under power. On such occasions the ride rapidly

became un-nerving for the peaky power, combined with wheels that did not always follow the contour of the road, would have machine and rider across the highway quicker than that.

In the process of delivering all that power the engine consumed fuel at a prodigious rate. The factory talked of 78 mpg at 31 mph but this was a joke to all who rode the model. Anything over 30 mpg was to be rated good or rider not trying and one tester got to 24 mpg during an Autoroute ride at speeds between 90 and 110 mph. A useful aid to the machine's ability to cruise at high speed were the really good brakes to halt it for the frequent fuel stops. Neither had much feel but they worked well from high or low speed.

The centre stand was poor and it needed a gorilla to pull the machine onto it but it was a motorcycle made for riding not sitting still. It represented a completely different image to the Honda CB750 that had been launched at the same time. The Honda with its 4 cylinders, electric start and disc brake was an equal performer but in a civilized manner that over the years was to become bland. The Mach III was never this but a fiery and outrageous road burner that was loved or hated to about the same degree. No-one was left unmoved by it.

For all its performance it did offer a Jeckyll and Hyde life. If the engine speed was kept down to around 5500 it became a docile multi that would run about town happily without fuss or temperament. It started very easily hot or cold and was easy to ride.

Take it into the plus 6000 realm and the other side of its nature snapped into life. The straight cut transmission gears whined, the ring-ding in the pipes began its work and the creature wailed its way up to 8000 and a ton. It was motorcycling in capital letters at a level only the *aficionado* could comprehend. None who preached of safety, economy or ecology would ever understand it or the hold it could place on those who enjoyed its spell.

The performance of the H1 straight from the crate was enough to make it a contender for road racing and sprints and sure enough 1969 saw some of them running with success in such events. One nearly took its class in the Production TT that year but sadly the rider was unseated when in the lead and only having a few miles to go to the finish.

At the end of 1969 Kawasaki did what was expected of them and brought out the H1R, a road racing version of the standard machine. Such was the performance of the road model that not too much was needed to lift the power to 75 bhp at 9000 rpm, while the weight came down to 300 lb thanks to the removal of the road equipment.

In the engine the compression ratio went up to 7·5 : 1 and all three port timings were extended. Carburettors of 35 mm were fitted with different size main jets for left, centre and right units while on the exhaust side went expansion boxes. These were held to stubs, bolted to the cylinders, by pairs of tension springs and crossed over in front of the engine to keep the overall width down. All three terminated in long, small diameter tail pipes and one went on the left and two to the right.

The engine was lubricated by an oil pump with preset output which was supplemented by mixing oil in the petrol at a 20 : 1 ratio. Ignition was by battery and coil with the alternator and rectifier retained to keep the charge up to scratch. Thus much of the normal wiring was used along with three sets of points, condensers and coils.

Above **Operating the rear chain oiler on the H2, a job required every 200 miles in 1972. Oil was carried in a small tank behind battery**

Right **The Mach IV in 1973 H2A form**

A close set of gearbox ratios were fitted and the overall gearing was raised by the use of a much smaller rear wheel sprocket. The primary drive remained much as on the road machine but the clutch went outside into the air and so ran dry. It contained 10 sintered friction plates to transmit the power and a seal behind it kept the transmission oil inside the modified right engine cover.

The cycle parts looked similar to those of the H1 but most changed to some extent. The frame seemed little altered but the main top tubes were taken down from the rear of the tank to the fork pivot area to complete the main cradle loops and the top part of the sub-frame was the added item. The result continued to be fitted with telescopics at the front and pivoted fork at the rear, plus a hydraulic straight-line steering damper.

Details altered so the battery was carried in a small bracket hung on the right and the oil went in a cylindrical tank fixed above the rear fork pivot. The fuel tank was long, low and narrow but held more than the standard model and the seat was short with a hump. It sat on rubber washers and the footrests and clip-ons matched its racing purpose.

Both wheels had alloy rims and racing tyres, the front a 3·00 × 18 in. and the rear 3·50 × 18 in. A brief front mudguard was bolted to the fork legs and a briefer one at the rear fitted between the seat and the fork pivot. Both hubs were full width, light alloy affairs with interrupted cooling ribs. The front drum was fitted with two massive twin leading shoe brakes each with external adjustment tie-rod between cam levers and an air scoop to assist cooling. The lower cam lever was extended for the operating cable and these swept up from each side to a balance box from which a single cable ran to the handlebar lever with its adjuster.

It looked most impressive but in use failed to retard the machine very well. Despite this it was fitted to all the production H1R models to the end although often changed by owners for a disc. It was backed by a single leading shoe drum at the rear, also with air scoop, that worked as well as any racing rear could be expected to.

The three carburettors were equipped with starter jets and so a forest of six cables rose from them to a pair of junction boxes. From these, single cables ran to twistgrip and air lever on the bars. A neat touch was the provision of a trio of blanking caps for the carburettor intakes.

A mechanical rev-counter went onto a bracket ahead of the headstock and the machine was supplied with a dolphin fairing. In the optional parts list were pedals to give a right gearchange and left brake, a Kawasaki emblem in choice of three colours and a plug spanner. More useful were alternative sprockets, a range of main jets and a portable stand.

It quickly proved to be competitive with a 7th in the prestigious Daytona race early in 1970. That year it had several good placings in the classics and from these Ginger Molloy finished

Right **The 1973 S2A, 350 cc and disc front brake, a good stopper**

Below **Six cylinders admire the view in Southern California (Lake Elsinor?), a 1974 H1E on the left and a 1973 H2A**

Above **750 cc triple at Daytona in 1973 fitted with cast alloy wheels and discs front and rear but still with patterned tyres, not slicks**

Left **A 1974 H2B pictured in California nine years later, nice condition, very original, but at $600 or offer, undervalued**

Above **Engine unit of the 1974 400 cc S3 which replaced the S2A. Cylinder head fins altered and engine rubber mounted**

Right **1974 H1E with revised CDI and check valves added to crankcase, still a real flyer**

second to Agostini in the 500 cc world championship. An outright win eluded it in 1970 but in the final grand prix in 1971 Dave Simmonds gave the firm their first 500 cc classic win at Jamara in Spain.

In time the racing 500 became the H1RA and in this form it developed 80 bhp at 9500 rpm on an 8·0:1 compression ratio. The port timing was extended further and it was fitted with CDI to fire the plugs. This system was powered by the alternator so the battery was dispensed with but the wiring was complex with three electronic boxes each with six leads. Two from each went to a coil and three to the generator and the trigger while the sixth connected to a kill switch unit which in turn was coupled by a single wire to an engine stop switch.

The racer continued in use in the early 1970s and took a number of classic placings in that period. It was not until 1975 that it gained another classic when Mick Grant won the Senior TT but by then it was the H1RW and a works machine. It had water-cooling, a 6-speed gearbox, cast alloy wheels and disc brakes but still showed its origins.

The H1R was only built up to 1971 and within its limitations of being based on a production model it was very competitive as its classic placings showed. However it would seem that Kawasaki moved away from it at the right time as the TZ Yamaha was not far below the horizon and later came the RG Suzuki, both machines being purpose built for racing. By then Kawasaki themselves had moved on with periods in formula 750, endurance, and later the 250 and 350 cc classes in all of which they were successful. Their return to the 500 cc class many years later was to be based on a totally different concept.

Meanwhile on the road the H1 continued through 1969 in its original tank and side cover colours of white or peacock grey but this was changed for 1970 to candy red. The contrasting tank stripe also altered as did the markings on the side covers. 1971 saw it become the H1A with a new style of petrol tank, a new candy blue colour and new styling lines to tank and side covers. These included the figure 500 to distinguish the capacity and this move heralded the introduction of a whole family of triples, all based on the same conception as the Mach III.

Two were smaller, these being the 250 cc S1 sold as the Mach I or 250-SS and the 350 cc S2 sold as the Mach II or 350-SS. The third was larger and was the 750 cc H2. In line with all the others it was exported as the Mach IV and marketed in Japan as the 750-SS. Thus Kawasaki had a pair of machines to supersede the A series twins and a model that met the Honda CB750 in its own capacity class and walked away from it at the traffic lights.

The two S models were based on a common bottom half with a 52·3 mm stroke. Bore of the S1 was 45 mm to give a 249·5 cc capacity while the S2 was 53 mm and 346 cc. That aside, the two models were very similar and without the side cover markings it was hard to tell them apart. Both had a 7·3:1 compression ratio but the port timings did vary by a few degrees and the carburettor sizes were 22 mm and 24 mm for the 250 and 350. The air cleaner differed from the H1 type but was still connected by moulded hose to all three units.

Internally the engines were much as the H1 with minor variations. The lubrication system had the pump bolted to the side of the right transmission cover and driven by a plastic spur gear that meshed with a small pinion on the end of the crankshaft. A spiral gear was attached to the plastic one and drove the rev-counter shaft run in the cover with a connection for the cable. The oil system was superlube with the three pipes from the pump connected to a check valve which passed the lubricant into the inlet tract. A notch was cut in each big end eye of the connecting rods to enable the oil mist to reach the bearings.

Ignition was by battery and coil with the three pairs of points mounted on the left outboard of

Above **The engine of the 1974 H1E**

Right **A 1974 H1E modified for production racing by removing the lights and centre stand and adding a small fairing. The star on the tank indicates some success has been gained**

Opposite **The H2B from 1974, first year with the hydraulic steering damper and the only year it was on the right**

the alternator. The result was 32 bhp at 8000 rpm from the S1 and 45 bhp at the same engine speed from the S2. It was transmitted via spur gears to a multiplate clutch and thence to a 5 speed gearbox, all very much as on the H1. Unlike the larger machine, neutral went between first and second gear and the two S models shared the same internal ratios and output sprocket size. The overall gearing was varied by the use of different rear wheel sprockets and the 350 also had a rear tyre of slightly greater section and a heavier grade of drive chain.

Machine features were similar to the 500 but the frame differed although it was built on the same lines, fitted with a pivoted fork and internal spring telescopic front forks with a friction steering damper. Both brakes were smaller than those fitted to the H1 with dimensions of 180 mm diameter and 30 mm width, and the twin leading shoes were retained at the front. The dimensions of the two S models varied a little with the wheelbase of the 350 a little shorter than that of the 250. The larger machine was heavier by 5 lb.

One feature shared by the S machines and not found on the 500 was a tail section formed by a moulding that ran from the back of the seat to the tail light which it supported. Access to this space was gained by lifting the seat and it provided a useful compartment for the stowage of tools and small items. One feature lost by them was the vacuum petrol tap, for a manual one was provided.

Performance of the Mach I was quoted as 104 mph with a standing quarter in 14·7 seconds while the figures for the S2 were 112 mph and 13·6 seconds. The speeds were perhaps optimistic just as with the H1 and the A series twins but there was no doubt that the two smaller triples were fast machines. Like the H1 they were fun to ride with the power coming in above 6000 rpm but without the harshness of the bigger model. They were more controllable, even more civilized, but could not be thought of as docile motorcycles.

The reduction in power and lower power to weight ratio did make a real change in the way

Above **The 1975 H2C, damper on left and new colour and markings**

1975 S1C still with drum front brake, a fast 250

The 1975 S3 with disc front, much faster and an exhilarating if thirsty ride

The 1975 H1F with the same marking as the very similar 750

the machines behaved on the road for 45 bhp is much easier to contain and the results of an abrupt throttle snap less startling. The S models certainly took off down the road in fine manner but without the vicious suddenness that was so common with the 500.

They proved just as thirsty as the Mach III with the S2 able to reach the nadir of consumption for a road model with a mere 19 miles being covered to digest one English gallon. This was achieved by cruising at full throttle into the wind at 100 mph plus speeds but the same machine did return 52 mpg when commuting. Few Kawasaki triples were ridden to achieve such a figure for it was a machine for riding, not to go anywhere, but just to be out on the road savouring the performance and the style in which it was delivered.

Faults it had and one concerned the front brake which worked well under heavy lever pressure when cold but got too hot and was in need of ventilation, a larger diameter and a change of lining material. For an 80 mph model it was fine, but for one able to top 105 and which asked to be ridden far and fast, it was not enough. Front suspension was soft and rear hard so the resulting inbalance had an effect on the handling but for all that it was good and only became a little frayed at the outer limits.

The testers of the day liked the triple and praised the good finish, sensible minor controls and quiet exhaust, although the rattle of the straight cut primary gears was still there. The 250 was not as exciting as the 350 but it still performed well and had the characteristic dual personality of the triple. Kept below 6000 it was an easy starting, docile commuter and tourer. Exceed the magic figure and off it shot looking and behaving just like the sports model it had become.

The third new model for 1971 was a very different story indeed for this was the Mach IV. It

came, it saw, it conquered and brought a whole new dimension to performance on the road straight from the crate. Suddenly, anyone could put down their cash and turn in 12 second standing quarters. Top speed was 126 mph and came from a surfeit of 74 bhp at 6800 rpm.

The machine was very similar to the H1 but stretched out to 71 × 63 mm and 748 cc. Compression ratio was 7·0:1, carburettors 30 mm diameter and the port timing very much as the 500. Ignition was capacitor discharge but powered by a magneto and not the battery. Due to the inherent characteristics of the triggering it had automatic electronic ignition advance. Lubrication and the oil pump were as the H1.

The transmission was as for the smaller triple but with altered ratios in gearbox and primary drive. The latter was raised considerably from 2·41 to 1·88 to reduce the torque into the clutch and gearbox but meant that the clutch ran faster. To keep the drum fingers from spreading, a steel band was fitted round the outside of the drum between the first and second friction plates.

The gearbox was modified to withstand the increased power and torque with fewer teeth in the top gear pair although the ratio remained the same. Fourth ratio was as on the Mach III, second and third lower but first was slightly higher. The final drive had more teeth at the rear wheel, an

Above **The works 500 cc triple in 1975 with water cooling, six speeds and cast wheels**

Right **The 750 cc three as raced in 1975 by the factory, also water cooled with cast magnesium alloy wheels and disc brakes**

endless chain and a small guard. As on the H1 the gearbox sequence had neutral below first gear but the changes to the bottom half of the engine were reflected in a small increase in transmission oil. An unusual feature was a manual chain oiler with its own reservoir which was required to be operated every 200 miles.

Chassis details were much as for the 500 but the frame was further braced and the forks used less damping oil. Only a friction steering damper was fitted and the tyre sizes remained as on the smaller triple. The petrol tank, still with automatic tap, was a couple of litres larger, while the oil tank was slightly smaller and the overall dimensions were little changed although the wheelbase was up a trifle. Ground clearance was greater and weight up to 423 lb with a distribution of 45/55 per cent front to rear.

Totally new was the front brake which was a disc with a working diameter of 245 mm and outside one of 296 mm. It went on the left side of the hub to which it was bolted with the caliper mounted ahead of the fork leg. The caliper was actuated by a hydraulic master cylinder mounted on the right handlebar, controlled by the front brake lever. It contained a single working piston and the body slid on two bolts to bring the second pad into contact with the disc and the hose line contained a pressure switch to turn on the stop light. At the rear went a conventional Kawasaki single leading shoe drum brake 200 mm diameter and 35 mm wide. The speedometer drive was retained at the front wheel on the left.

In appearance and styling the Mach IV copied its smaller S series brothers with the same tail

Above **Final 500 cc triple, the KH500-A8 in 1976 with revised gearshift pattern, less power and other changes**

Right **Publicity photo of 1976 KH250-B1 with disc front brake and model Tina Johnson ready to button her shirt**

Above **The Kawasaki triples were tailormade for 'caféizing'—this is one of Read Titan's efforts on the 750 with fresh tank, seat and additional fairing, rearsets and Ace bars**

Left **Posed publicity shot of 1977 KH400-A4, a fast and thirsty motorcycle**

Above **The KH250-B4 from 1979, nearly the last year and only changed in colour and graphics**

Left above **Riding the smallest triple in 1978 when the model code was KH250-B3**

section behind the seat with its small stowage compartment, front mudguard painted to match the tank and side cover colour and the same swoopy tank lining continued onto the tail section.

It was a very handsome motorcycle and only came in pearl candy blue. It also had a frightening performance for more power, high wide bars and weight to the rear meant that the front end came up as if it was geared to the twistgrip. The riding position made a 12 seconds dead time for the quarter very hard to achieve as it was difficult to make the back tyre break traction to get real drive onto the road. All too often it gripped and the torque just turned it skywards.

It was like the H1 but more so. In 1971 the idea of so much raw power in a low weight package really stirred the adrenalin when coupled with the Mach III reputation. The IV just had to be an over-the-top exercise that was pure evil. And so it was marked down which was perhaps a little unfair for Kawasaki had done a fair job of containing the high performance in a chassis that coped well for the times and the then existing state of the art. A decade later and it would not startle but when it emerged it set a new standard for decadent performance.

It went, it smoked, it guzzled petrol, it vibrated and the engine wailed over a massive power band that ran from 3500 to past the red line. It was really all too much but in many ways behaved better than the 500. The handling was generally held to be better, the disc brake worked, the right fork was lugged to take a second disc for the really hard, fast men, and a good number of useful features were built in.

But it was never quite the success or really gained the affection the 500 won. Somehow the slightly lower speed but more twitchy handling plus the peaky power output caught the imagination and was preferred. The 750 suffered from the faults inherent in a triple to a degree that put it over the edge for many. For blasting from the lights it was the tool of the year but even that required considerable finesse or a new pair of low, flat handlebars.

The road testers drooled over the performance and lauded the undoubted excitement of riding the machine but for all that it really was an expensive luxury and power overkill so many preferred the CB750 or, if they sought a 2-stroke triple, chose the Suzuki GT750 as being more civilized and more of a tourer. Not that the Mach IV would not tour and be servile, just that the rider never let it behave that way—it was too irresistable.

So Kawasaki had four versions of the triple to run with in 1972 and better facilities with which to make, sell and service them. Parts handling had been improved in 1971 by the creation of a computerized warehouse for them at the Akashi works and in 1972 an engineering centre was established at the same plant. Abroad in Columbia they began knockdown production with Auto Tecnica Columbiana that same year so that motorcycle production was now very big Kawasaki business indeed and far from its early tentative days.

No longer did two wheelers fill a production gap to keep a factory working and the company name was now very well established and known worldwide for its performance machines.

For 1972 the S1, S2 and H2 continued without change while the 500 became the H1B. It took the tank style and markings of the other models plus other changes. The complex battery powered electronic ignition was dropped in favour of conventional coils with triple sets of points mounted on the left and controlled by a single cam on the end of the crankshaft. The surface discharge plugs were changed for the more normal type, albeit of a hard grade.

The other changes affected the front end with revised front forks, a straight-line hydraulic steering damper in addition to the friction one and a single disc brake. This was the same as used on the H2 and thus relieved an overstressed component which retired gratefully, bowing out to the newer technology. Riders were happier too; they could now stop with the pack at corner after corner. In the change-over the front mudguard lost its stays and much of its length behind the fork legs.

1973 saw all the models change their colour and marking with the usual Kawasaki suffix letter tacking onto the model type. The S1A went to a chrome plated front mudguard as did the S2A and both were fitted with new seats. The larger model also received the revised front forks and disc front brake as on the 500 but with a slightly smaller 277 mm diameter.

The Mach III went through a brief H1C phase when it reverted to battery powered electronic ignition and a fork variation with much less damping oil. It then became the H1D with the magneto electronic ignition system from the H2 firing its standard plugs. Power dropped a touch to 59 bhp at 8000 rpm and the weight went up to 408 lb. Reasons were an increase in tank capacity, new seat, the addition of the seat tail stowage compartment and longer chrome plated front mudguard while other changes were an endless rear chain, forks as used on the H1C and a steering head angle 2 degrees steeper. Top speed was now quoted as 112 mph.

The 750 became the H2A with the same mudguard changes in length and finish as on the H1 while the engine was fitted with an oil pump with reduced output.

At the end of 1973 the S2 was replaced by the slightly larger S3 so Kawasaki continued with four triples. The new model was based on the old but bored out to 57 mm and 400·4 cc. It ran on a 6·5:1 compression ratio and was fed by a trio of 26 mm carburettors to produce 42 bhp at 7000 rpm, rather less than the 350. Port timings were either the same or within a couple of degrees and ignition was still by points.

The engine unit was rubber mounted to the frame to reduce the effects of vibration and inside the unit the bottom half and the transmission remained the same although the overall gearing was raised. The frame had a longer wheelbase and the front tyre was a trifle wider at a 3·25 in. section. The front brake was a single disc on the left with the caliper ahead of the fork leg. Effective diameter was 226 mm and outside diameter 277 mm. At the rear went the usual Kawasaki single leading shoe drum of 180 mm diameter and 30 mm width.

The S3 was in a new marking used throughout the triple range and the colours for each model were changed. Its new seat was also used on the S1B and both had brake wear indicators added where drums were used. On the smaller model the friction steering damper was discontinued and it shared the longer wheelbase with the S3.

For the H series the 500 became the H1E with revised chassis, new type electronic ignition, rubber engine mounts and check valves. These last were added to each crankcase base to remove any oil that drained into that area and pass it to one of the main bearings. The same arrangement went onto the H2B which also received a longer wheelbase and a straight line hydraulic steering damper.

The new 400 was a 100 mph motorcycle and offered much the same performance as the S2 and in similar vein. It was more docile than the 500 and so easier to use in give-and-take situations. The raw edges were gradually being honed away and with their going went some of the charisma of the model type.

1975 brought colour and marking changes only to the S1C, S3A and H1F but the H2C had other alterations as well. The in-line steering damper moved onto the left and the lubrication system changed. Instead of feeding oil into the inlet tracts it was piped into the float chambers to combine with the petrol and flow into the engine with the mixture. It thus fed the piston and some mains via drain holes but the big ends continued with their pumped supply via the other mains as in the past. In addition the flywheel shape was altered to part round or pork chop and this move reduced the primary compression ratio. Power dropped to 71 bhp.

Late in the year the S1C was fitted with larger section tyres which made them common with the 400. For 1976 model designations all altered to the KH type with the smallest machine becoming the KH250-A5. In this form it adopted a 3 fuse system to protect the electrics, new bar grips and a locking petrol tank cap. Colour and markings were new for the year with the latter common to the triple range.

Next in size was the KH400-A3 with the power down to 38 bhp at 7000 rpm, revised carburettor settings, softer sparking plugs, CDI and the items used by the 250. Unlike that model the 400 had a disc front brake and that was fitted with water resistant pads. The same pads went onto the KH500-A8 which was fitted with the 3 fuses, new grips and tank lock but of more interest to riders was a change to the gear selection pattern to put neutral between first and second.

Power output was down to 52 bhp at 7000 rpm with a heart shaped inlet port without a bridge and in this form the 500 had lost the special appeal of the Mach III although it still remained a fast machine. For a time some riders compensated by fitting H1 barrels but once these dried up it was only possible to regain the power by expensive, specialized port work.

Similar problems beset owners of other sizes of the triple who sought to regain the power of the past. The old S1 could be bored to become a 350 but this was not possible with the S1A. A set of S2 parts were too costly to contemplate and the KH400 items did not fit the S1 range. Easier was engine swapping with the 250, 350 and 400 interchangeable as were the H1 and H2.

The H2C had been the last of the listed big triples but some did emerge as the KH750A to bring its days to an end. With the environmental set glowering at its smoky exhaust and vast consumption, the safety set whining about the wheelies and the ecologists plainly hating it, there were too many guns bearing on Kawasaki for them to support it. The point had been made anyway, the Mach series led their class, now big K was respectable and sold nice clean fours.

The final 250, the 1980 KH250-B5, with the colour and graphics changed again. Tee-shirt advertises Kawasaki's 1978 world championships in 250 and 350 cc classes. Note seat marking

If the 750 had to go the 250 stayed in the ring and was joined by a new series as the KH250-B1. The difference was the addition of a disc front brake and the use of the 400 cycle parts. This removed the handling variations of the S series where the 250 was neutral and the 400 fell into slow corners.

The 250 with either brake ran to about 85 mph but was easier to ride fast with the disc as this gave more confidence than the rather undersized drum. On the 400 it still gave confidence and helped the machine to cover ground very rapidly with its vivid acceleration, 100 mph top speed and stable handling. Comfort was adequate but anyway stops were frequent as fuel could be consumed at 30 miles to the English gallon.

The 500, now a little dated, was dropped at the end of 1976 as was the drum braked 250 but the other models continued as the KH250-B2 and KH400-A4 for 1977. Changes were now few, other than the usual colour and marking ones, to give a new line and style to each season. 1978 brought the B3 and A5 marks with a new brake master cylinder and seat while 1979 saw the B4 and A6 unchanged mechanically. And so it was for the final triple year in 1980 with the KH250-B5 and KH400-A7 reaching their last form and then vanishing to make way for a new breed of 4-strokes.

Their once startling performance had become commonplace with road 250s reaching close to the ton while their fuel consumption was no longer a joke in a world where petrol had become so expensive. The emission laws had chased them from their first and best market in the USA so Kawasaki did the sensible thing and pulled them from the range.

Already only a memory was the most outrageous of them, the racing 750 cc H2R which came on the scene in 1972. Like the 500 it was based on the road model and modified in similar manner to push the power up to 100 bhp plus at 9000 rpm. To stop it, a second disc was added

Kawasaki triple wearing Ian Dyson glasswork with special tank cover, seat base, tail and fairing of very sleek form. Special cast spoke wheels too

at the front and a larger drum at the rear, but this later changed to a disc. The early tyres copied the sizes used on the 500 but again, in time, changed to the wider slicks of the 1970s.

It was a quick, brutal racer and used by the works only who turned out with them finished in a lime green matched by their riders' leathers. Thanks to the colour and some early dubious handling, they quickly became known as the 'Green Meanies' and the nickname stuck long after they had the steering sorted out. The green colour stayed and made the machines some of the easiest to spot on the circuit.

The H2R was successful in America and later in Europe, even if something of a handful to ride. In many cases the chassis was used to house the H1R engine and in a few the reverse occurred, but that meant relying on drum brakes to bring the assembly to a halt. In 1975 the model became the water-cooled KR750 with cast alloy wheels and a good few other internal changes. It had a very good year which was repeated in 1976 but from then on faded apart from odd highlights.

The day of the big racing triple came to an end as the 500 cc fours developed as much power and were easier to handle. Like the road models, they were missed for their sheer raw excitement.

For the big triple on the road it was the end of the day but riders everywhere mourned the loss of that special something the ring-ding, whining, smoking three could produce as it twitched on its way with the torque pulling the wheels out of line and up into the sky.

7 'King of the road'—Z1

Full frontal power—the Z engine

The Kawasaki 2-stroke twins and triples established the company's name for performance in a brash manner. This was acceptable at first for the noise, the loud behaviour, the rawness, all grabbed attention and publicity fast and made the headlines. As they became known, this need grew less urgent and the brashness started to be an embarrassment so Kawasaki looked to a more dignified way to give the customer the best performance on the street.

This work began back in 1967 before the Mach III hit the market and was carried out under the code of NYS which stood for New York Steak. The aims of the machine were to carry on from the Big W series, to build on this to produce a model with more style and panache, to create a machine that not only gave the performance expected of a Kawasaki but that was superior to all the opposition, to present that performance in a refined and distinguished way, and to offer the whole in a tasteful package.

Research went into the market needs and the competition's models. The machine brief was worked on and firmed up to be a touring motorcycle with a surplus of power for hauling very full equipment as needed. Good handling was required as run solo the machine's performance was bound to be sporting thanks to the power sought. The machine was to be well equipped, built to high standards and to create the minimum pollution. All current and predicted future emission standards were to be met.

From this work came the decision to build a 4-stroke, to build it big at 750 cc and to fit twin overhead camshafts to make the power easy to find. To provide the level of sophistication desired four cylinders would be needed.

In 1968 design work began and mock-ups were built. Engineering and styling teams worked on their problems and gradually the parts began to fall into place. Kawasaki looked happily ahead to the 1970s when their new four would run alongside the H1 triple they were just about to launch on an unsuspecting public.

It dropped onto the market in September 1968 with the subtlety of a bomb but any satisfaction the firm had was wiped out totally in October. That month saw Honda announce their CB750 at the Tokyo motor show and it had virtually all the features of the Kawasaki. Bland oriental faces were kept shut tight during the show and the NYS project stopped dead in its wheeltracks.

Once the initial shock had worn off, Kawasaki began to think again and realised that just maybe the CB750 was not such a bad thing. They could now see what the market reaction was to a big transverse four in practice, study the machine, read test reports, pull one or more to pieces and then re-appraise the market with the advantage of knowing what they had to beat.

The CB750 was a runaway success and well it deserved to be. For the first time an overhead camshaft four with 5-speed gearbox and disc front brake was readily on sale world-wide. Earlier attempts to market such models had always been by specialists and the results expensive and few in number. The big Honda was available everywhere with full service back-up and in a very short time they were to be seen on the roads in large numbers.

Kawasaki watched this happen and it was very apparent that there was a market for another big four so in the autumn of 1969 they made their decision. The NYS project was on again very much in its original concept but upgraded to out-do the Honda. To this end the capacity was increased to 900 cc and the power output was expected to be a good deal higher than that of the CB750. Production was to begin in 1972 and meanwhile Kawasaki owners could annoy the big Honda with the Mach III. In 1971 they would get the Mach IV to really crush the opposition and if then taken to task for using such a raw, brutal tool could finally turn to the svelte new four.

Early in 1970 styling sketches were drawn up in profusion seeking to give the image of a lightweight sprinter with low, easy riding seat despite the size and bulk inherent in the sheer capacity of the engine. It was also imperative that the result looked different to the Honda. From this early exercise came a trial model, more sketches, mock-ups and even more sketches. Mid-year a project team was formed with engine and chassis specialists and their task was aided by the earlier work already carried out for the 750.

By the end of the year the prototype was well advanced and in the spring of 1971 it ran at the Yatabe test circuit. There were problems. The breather system sprayed oil out instead of keeping it in, the piston crowns wilted, detail parts had to be tested, modified and re-tested but one by one the troubles were dealt with and problems eradicated. Encouragement came in the form of 95 bhp from one of the prototypes and a test run timed at over 140 mph.

Kawasaki nerves could relax a little, the four was going to work. With the USA the major market, the next phase of testing was on the roads of that country and early in 1972 two machines were sent to Los Angeles. They covered a large mileage each day at high speed and suffered many gruelling tests. About the toughest was a trip from LA to Daytona and back with stop-offs en route to run on race courses. The chains wore out but not much else and the machines went back to Japan for a full check out.

They returned once more to the USA for final trials and then in June 1972 many of the world's motorcycle press were invited to Japan. They were

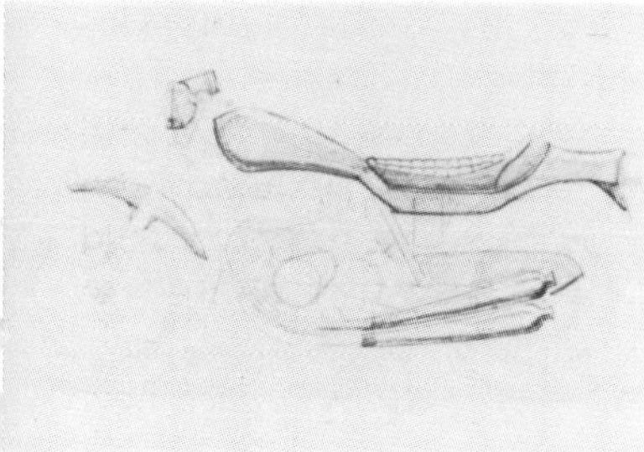

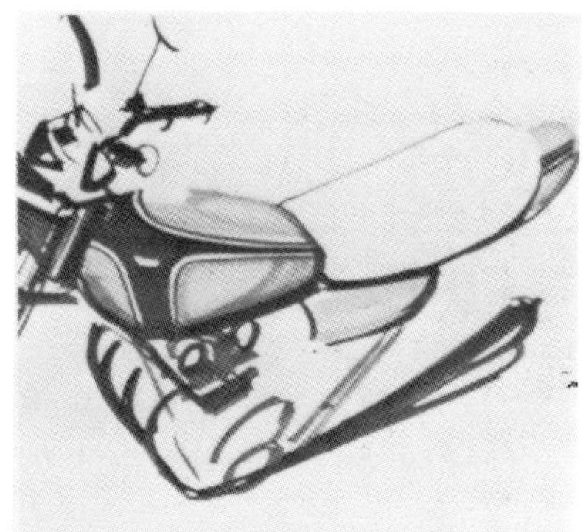

A series of early design sketches for the NYS, *in top line*, **followed by a more detailed machine drawing,** *left of line 2*, **a mock-up based on the early ideas,** *centre*, **and a prototype whose trimmings are not finalized on the** *right*. *Below, right* **is a graphic sketch of an alternative version and** *left* **a complete machine nearly as launched. Tank decor was changed again and DOHC moved off clutch cover**

shown the machine and their opinions and criticisms sought. Production had begun in the previous month but at a low level to cover the initial launch needs.

In September 1972 the Z1 was launched at the Cologne Show, one of the most important in Europe. Mass production got underway at the same time but at a steady 1500 units per month while the market reaction was awaited. Kawasaki's initial caution was soon to be swept away in a flood of orders and by 1975 production was running at 5000 per month. In part, this was thanks to a 4-stroke assembly factory completed in October 1972.

The German show was followed by exhibitions in Paris, Oslo and, in November, Earls Court where Agrati gave the Z1 its UK debut. Quickly, the model went on sale world-wide and as quickly they were snapped up by eager customers. Kawasaki at first called it the Bike of Bikes but before long the press and public had their own name for it which stuck. It was the King and wore its crown well for many a year.

This machine, a real superbike, was based on

Right **The 750 cc Z2 built for the Japanese home market and nearly identical to the 900**

Below **The King, the 900 cc Z1 in its original form. Twin overhead camshafts, four exhausts, disc front, fast and furious**

a clever blend of advanced engineering and practical features. Thus, although it had twin overhead camshafts, it was essentially easy enough to service. With the engine still installed in the frame the cylinder head and block could be removed as could items such as the generator, starter, clutch and gearchange mechanism. Only if the crankshaft or gearbox required attention was it necessary to take the engine unit out and this was a simple if weighty task.

The engine was the heart of the machine giving it its power, performance and style. It was also quiet, docile and happy to run on regular fuel grades. It was equally at home pottering, as it was past the red-line. The unit was cast in the mould of the standard in-line four with the outer pistons moving together in opposition to the two centre ones. As was usual practice the crankcase split horizontally on the crankshaft centre line and contained the 5-speed gearbox.

Bore and stroke of the engine were equal at 66 mm and the capacity was 903 cc. The crankshaft assembly was an all caged roller affair with a total of six main bearings supporting it with the central pair clamped to the upper crankcase half by a bearing cap held by four bolts. The crankshaft was pressed together with the mainshafts forged with the webs and these shaped to provide the balance factor. The two outer mains could be pulled off and changed but if any of the other four or any of the big ends failed it meant a replacement crankshaft. In time it

Above **The Z1 on the Agrati stand at Earls Court in November 1972 when it was launched in the UK to an enthusiastic reception**

Left **An early Z1 in the USA during a *Cycle World* test. The same lines were used for 1972 and 1973**

became known that this was a rare occurrence given clean oil and filters and the rollers happily turned on a nice low oil pressure.

With a built-up crankshaft one piece rods could be and were used. They carried domed pistons on gudgeon pins retained by circlips and each piston was fitted with one scraper and two compression rings. The pistons gave a compression ratio of 8·5:1 and ran in iron sleeves cold pressed into the light alloy block. A flange at the top located each sleeve which extended down below crankcase level to support the piston.

The block had a tunnel cast into its centre for the camshaft drive chain and a total of 12 studs ran up through it from the crankcase, two carrying hollow location dowels. On top went the light alloy cylinder head and like the block this was well finned and painted black for good heat radiation and a smart appearance. The valve seats were cast in the head and made in an extra hard material to allow the use of lead free fuel without harmful effects.

The valves moved in pressed-in bronze guides and this material proved to be one of the few mistakes Kawasaki engineers made. It wore too fast for comfort and in later years was changed for iron, this becoming the stock replacement for all Z1 engines. Each guide was located by a circlip and carried an oil seal to bear against the valve stem. Each valve was held to its seat by duplex coil springs and these had their own seat fitted round the guide and were retained by a collar and split collets.

The head casting included the individual ports for each cylinder and at the rear each inlet had an intake hose with flange secured by two screws. These intakes were of composite construction with a hard flange bonded to the hose which carried an external clip for clamping it to the carburettor. The hose moulding also carried a pipe for connection to a vacuum gauge for synchronization purposes following a minor problem with the early models which had the pipes in the cylinder head. On the front of the head each exhaust port was flanked by a pair of studs on which fitted a finned pipe collar. This went against a split flanged collar which in turn held the exhaust pipe against its gasket in the port. By this method the various parts could be removed over the flange on the end of the pipe.

The head casting also contained the lower part of the cambox with its top surface on the camshaft centre line. The two shafts were positioned above their respective valves and each of these was moved by a lifter interposed between it and the cam. Each lifter carried a shim in its top and valve clearances were adjusted by changing these which ranged in thickness from 2·00 to 3·20 mm in 0·05 mm steps. The lifters ran directly in bores machined into the head and surrounded the valve springs.

Each camshaft ran in four pairs of split plain bearings. These were positioned in two assemblies between each end cam and the next one inboard and the two top shells halves of each assembly held by a single housing fixed by four bolts and located by two dowels. There were thus four top housings each dealing with two bearings and with a cam either side of them. Between one pair of bearings the camshaft was machined with two rings of increased diameter to locate it sideways. The end cams were thus overhung and both camshafts were flanged in the centre to enable the drive sprockets to be bolted to them. The exhaust camshaft was also machined with a skew gear to drive the rev-counter.

The head was held down by 12 nuts on the studs screwed into the crankcase assisted by a single additional bolt at each end. When in place with the camshafts these were enclosed by a single top cover of H pattern that ran over each shaft and the central tunnel. At the end of each cambox the wall was machined away in a half circle to allow the bearing housings to be finished and the resulting holes were blanked off with half round bungs. They were to remain a feature of the engine type.

Above **Sales leaflet for the 1975 Z1B with revised colour and markings, new type of rear chain and no chain oiler**

Right **USA advert for the Z1B which followed the company theme of the time—'lets the good times roll'**

The sparking plugs inclined out from the centre of the engine and air flow past them and between the camboxes was enhanced by the head fins which were angled to force it to the middle.

The camshafts were driven by a single endless chain from the centre of the crankshaft where a sprocket was cut. Various rollers, guides and sprockets kept its tension correct and ensured it followed its prescribed path. Lowest of these was a roller set on a spindle in the top surface of the crankcase with the chain passing either side of it. Above this in the block tunnel went a fixed guide at the front, and at the top of the block there were two sprockets, both in fixed positions to increase the chain wrap at the camshaft sprockets. Below the rear one and pivoted about it went a roller with a spring behind it to control the chain tension.

The chain then ran out to the camshafts and across the head between them but with one more sprocket in that run to take the chain down a little. By this means it again increased the wrap a trifle and was itself mounted in a bracket held

to the head with rubber damping to play its part in removing any tendency for the chain to vibrate.

The camshafts were marked and despite the presence of two of them, it was a straightforward job to set the timing, alter the valve clearances or remove the cylinder head.

The two crankcase halves were large light alloy castings split on the centre line through crankshaft and both gear shafts. The bearing housings were all machined with the halves assembled and a series of pins and half rings located the bearings radially and axially. The main bearings were all fitted into housings and each of the six were fixed by a pin to ensure alignment of the oil holes. The two centre mains were clamped by a single housing cap which bolted up to the top half but the other four were clamped by the lower case half as were the four gearbox bearings.

The underside of the lower case was open and sealed off by an oil pan held in place by numerous bolts. This was also an alloy casting and it had a large hole in its centre, sealed with an O ring, into which the oil filter was set.

The lubrication system was wet sump and dealt with the needs of engine, gearbox and primary transmission with a single gear type pump. This was located low down in the sump with a large gauze filter on its underside. The upper pump gear shaft carried a large spur gear and this was driven directly from the crankshaft. The drive gear was cut into the mainshaft between the first and second cylinders on the left.

The oil went from the pump to the filter with its replaceable element and beside this was positioned a by-pass valve. From the filter a drilling led to the main distribution passage from which the oil took three paths. The first led to each of the six main bearings and via them the four big ends and the starter clutch gear. Oil escaping from all these points lubricated the cylinders, pistons and plain small ends by splash. The second path was up through the block to the cambox and into the camshafts to emerge at the bearings and then to lubricate the cams and fall over the lifters. Drains from their recesses and the chain tunnel allowed the oil to fall back to the sump.

Route number three was to the gearbox bearings and all oil fell back to the sump after it had done its job. The main oil feed also connected to a pressure switch bolted in a well set in the top of the upper crankcase half and beside this went the engine breather.

This was part of what Kawasaki called PCV, or positive crankcase ventilation, which was a system used by many car engines to reduce emissions. Engine breathing in a four is not a great problem as the under piston displacement remains nearly constant but emission control needed some attention. The problem arose from piston blowby where raw fuel slipped past the rings into the crankcase and needed to be removed before it contaminated the oil but without passing it out to the open air.

To prevent this the breather assembly was mounted on top of the crankcase and the gas pumped out was fed by hose to the air cleaner box where it was inhaled into the engine and burnt. The result was a very significant reduction in hydrocarbon emissions.

The carburettors were four VM28 Mikuni units with throttle slides and separate starter circuits. They were all mounted to one plate and so could be fitted or removed as a complete assembly. The four slides were connected to a cross-rod and this controlled their movement and was turned by the twistgrip via two cables. Thus the rider had positive control and even if the return spring broke could still close the throttles. Once set in synchronization, all four were adjusted for tickover speed by a single throttle stop screw. The four starter circuits were also linked by a cross-rod and this terminated in a lever on the left for the rider to move.

The carburettors had stub ends front and rear which were clamped into the intake hoses and onto which the air cleaner hoses were pushed. These were part of a large single moulding containing the air filter which was accessible from under the seat.

Ignition was by conventional coil and battery with two sets of points under a cover at the right end of the crankshaft. A centrifugal advance mechanism was keyed to it and carried a single lobe cam which opened each pair of points once per engine revolution. This fired a double ended coil to the pair of cylinders whose pistons were at the top of their stroke so the system operated

Left **Final year of the 900 was 1976 when the Z900-A4 was built with dual front discs and audible turn signals**

Right **Brochure picture (English market) of Z900 which had smaller carburettors but was otherwise little changed from the Z1**

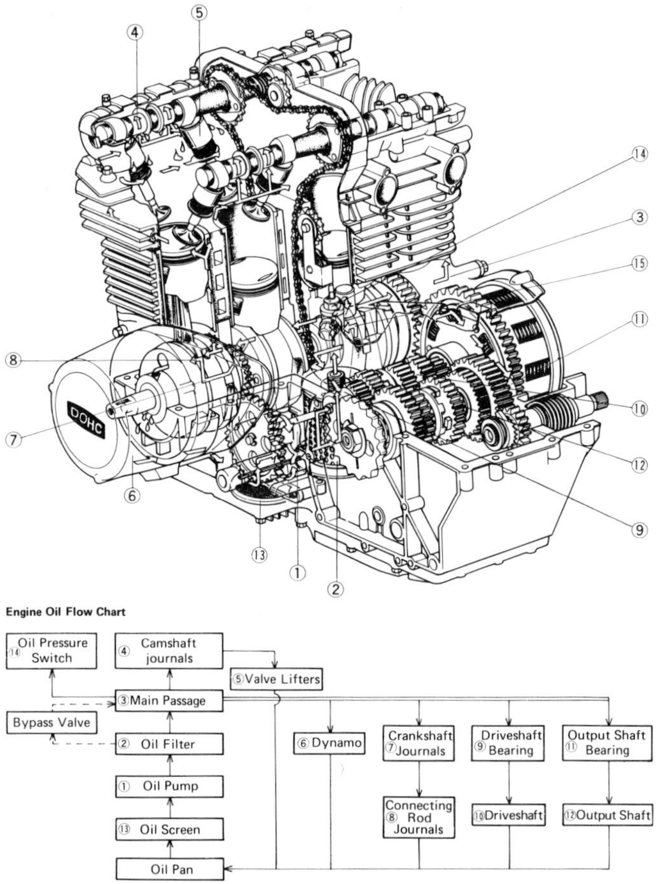

Line drawing of complete engine and gearbox unit detailing lubrication system with oil flow chart below

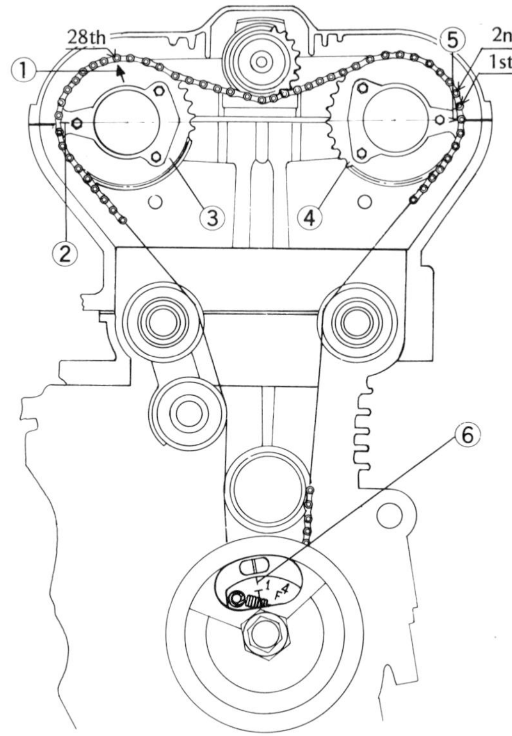

1. 28th Pin Mark
2. Timing Mark
3. Inlet Camshaft Sprocket
4. Exhaust Camshaft Sprocket
5. Timing Mark
6. #1, 4 TDC Mark

Line drawing of camshaft drive shows the various jockey wheels, sprockets and the timing procedure

on the lost spark principle as is common with Japanese machines.

The Z1 was fitted with an electric starter and this item was mounted on top of the crankcase to the rear of the left cylinders under a cover. It was a conventional direct current motor and sealed to a casting extension of the crankcase behind the left end of the crankshaft. Its spindle end was cut with gear teeth to form a pinion and meshed with an idler gear pair that drove a large gear fitted behind the alternator. This contained a one way clutch so that while the starter could turn the engine over, once this ran the gear train ceased to turn. Current for the starter was supplied via a relay and this was controlled by a button on the right handlebar.

The transmission of the big Kawasaki was very simple and involved the minimum number of gears, shafts, bearings and potential points for friction. Primary transmission was a spur gear pair with the two gears produced in the easiest way. At the front the gear was cut in the metal of the inner web of the right cylinder so was an inherent part of the crankshaft. Behind, the second gear ran on a needle race mounted on the gearbox input shaft and drove the clutch drum via shock absorbing springs.

The clutch was multi-plate with 8 friction and 7 plain all clamped up by 5 springs. The plates were separated by a quick-thread mechanism on the left, a push rod through the mainshaft and a mushroom against the pressure plate. The complete assembly lived under a cover on the right side of the engine and could be dismantled while in the machine expect for the removal of the clutch drum itself. That required the crank-case to be split but all else including the drive hub came out easily enough.

The gearbox was all indirect with 5 speeds and cross-over drive. Ball races supported the shafts behind the clutch and final drive sprocket with needle bearings at the other ends. The five gears were arranged in the order 2, 5, 3, 4, 1 from the left and various sizes of gear tooth form were used to enable the desired number of teeth, and hence the ratios to be obtained. Thus 2nd and 3rd output gears both had 35 teeth but meshed with 16 and 21 tooth input gears while the 4th input also had 21 teeth but ran with 29 on the output.

Gear selection was by three forks, one of which ran on the barrel cam and the other two on a separate cross-rod with pins engaging in the cam tracks. Both lay beneath the gearbox shafts and the barrel cam emerged on the left with 6 pins in its end. These were pulled as required by the positive stop mechanism and this terminated in the gear pedal on the left.

The gearbox contained two useful rider aids, one in the box proper and the other in the positive stop. The first comprised three ball bearings set inside 4th gear. When turning they flew out under centrifugal force and allowed the gear to slide axially for selection but when still at least one ball would drop into a slot in the shaft. This prevented the full selection occurring and the result was neutral easy to find from first gear and the mechanism could not move on into second.

The second aid was a second lever in the mechanism that rotated the cam drum. This was positioned to stop it moving further than intended under inertia forces no matter how quickly the rider moved the gear pedal. Small points but useful.

The machine was fitted with a kickstarter as well as the electric one and the lever was positioned on the right on a spindle to the rear of the clutch cover. A simple face ratchet turned a gear which meshed with first on the output shaft and hence with the crankshaft. A stop pulled the ratchet out of mesh when the pedal was returned to allow the gear to run free.

Final drive was by endless chain on the left and its driving sprocket sat in a chamber of its own. Inboard was the cover for the gearchange mechanism and outboard a protective sheet and then an outer cover. It was this that carried the clutch lifting mechanism and a further small cover gave access to the centre adjusting screw and locknut.

Behind this went a second oil pump driven by the gearbox output shaft and devoted to the good health of the rear chain. The pump was of the rotating plunger type with a variable output that could be adjusted by altering the plunger travel. The oil was carried in a small tank mounted under the seat and left the pump via a non-return valve which passed it into the gearbox shaft. There it was thrown out through holes onto the chain as the shaft turned.

The engine and gearbox of the Kawasaki was a substantial unit of considerable weight despite the extensive use of light alloy. It dominated the complete machine to play a large part in the final line and style with the four exhausts managing to set their individual stamp on it by looking very different to those of the CB750. To set the unit off the alternator cover carried the legend 'DOHC' as did the points cover after the pre-production models which had 'Kawasaki'. At an earlier stage the points cover had been blank and the 'DOHC' cast into the clutch one but in the end it was that cover which remained clean and unmarked of any decoration but fitted with a sight glass for checking the oil level.

Power output was 82 bhp at 8500 rpm, so well above that of the Honda, while peak torque was at 7000 rpm. In practice the torque was so massive that the machine would run down to 10 mph in top gear and pull away smoothly.

The complete unit was carried in a duplex cradle frame similar to that used for the triples. Twin tubes ran back from the base of the headstock to the rear of the tank where they curved down to the rear fork pivot. A single tube ran back from the top of the headstock to act as a brace and twin tubes ran down from a point just below it. They ran under the engine and up past the fork pivot to the rear damper mountings where they joined the top rear sub-frame loop.

The front forks were hydraulically damped telescopics with light alloy legs each with a split clamp end and a side reflector mounted at the top. The fork stanchions were held in both fork crowns by pinch bolts and the fork springs went inside them. Oil seals kept the damping fluid inside and dust seals kept the dirt off them without any help from gaiters. Between the fork crowns the stanchions were covered by shrouds that also carried the headlamp shell. The forks turned

1975 Z1B at rest. She wears Kawasaki style riding jacket

on ball races and no steering damper was fitted. Owners sometimes took the piston hydraulic damper from the H2 model and fitted that but as the frame bracket was too close to the bottom yoke, it would be snapped of on full lock.

At the rear went a pivoted fork with bushes to move on and this was controlled by a pair of hydraulically damped spring units. These had three positions of preload available to accommodate passengers and variations in rider weight and luggage.

Both wheels were built up with wire spokes and steel rims with the front fitted with a 3·25 × 19 in. tyre and the rear with a 4·00 × 18 in. The front brake was a 296 mm diameter disc fitted to the left side of the hub and the skew gear driven speedo cable went on the same side.

The disc was braked hydraulically with the master cylinder mounted on the right handlebar with the front brake lever. From it a flexible hose ran to a junction block bolted to the lower fork crown and this was fitted with a hydraulically operated front brake stop light switch. A further hose ran down to the fork leg where a brake pipe connected to the caliper assembly.

This only contained one working piston so the body together with the two brake pads had to be free to slide sideways on its two bolts. These ran through the holder plate and this was fixed to the leg by two further bolts. The right fork leg was also equipped with lugs to carry a caliper and the hub would accept a second disc so dual discs could be fitted if considered essential. Normally this was not so but for sidecar use or production racing a second disc was an asset.

At the rear a single leading shoe drum brake, 200 mm diameter and 35 mm wide, went into a full width, light alloy hub with cooling ribs. The hub was held in the frame on a single spindle but turned on three ball races with the sprocket bolted to a coupling which drove the hub through a series of shock absorber rubbers. The brake backplate was in light alloy with two pivot pins, one for each shoe, linked at their outer ends for greater rigidity. The plate extended down to pick up on the torque arm which ran forward to a point on the underside of the rear fork leg. The brake was rod operated by a pedal on the right and this was linked by a tension spring to a stop-light switch mounted on a bracket above it.

Both wheels were protected by chrome plated mudguards, the front one short and without stays, the rear longer and valanced. Above it the seat hinged up with a stay to keep it up while maintenance matters were dealt with and behind the seat went a tailbox running back to the rear light unit. A grab rail ran behind the seat and was bolted to the top fixings of the rear suspension units.

The petrol tank held 18 litres and was fitted with a manual tap with off, on and reserve postions, the last allowing the final 4 litres of fuel to reach the engine. The tap incorporated a fuel filter. Instruments were speedometer and revcounter mounted side by side in a combined housing. Between them went the ignition key and below this warning lights for neutral, oil pressure, main beam and turn signals.

The handlebars were clamped to the top fork crown and rose up high and it was not until 1975 and the Z1B that there was an option of a lower pair for the European market. The controls were conventional and the electric ones were placed with starter, kill and main lights switches on the right and horn, dip, pass and turn on the left.

Turn indicators were fitted and both bars carried rear view mirrors. Pillion footrests were hung from the frame loops that supported the silencers and both centre and prop stands were fitted.

In all it added up to 506 lb of very impressive motorcycle and it was finished in black with the tank in candy yellow or candy brown with side covers to match.

The Z1 received rave reviews from the World's motorcycle press as well it deserved, for it was the first of a new generation of extra large machines. It offered refined and sophisticated two-wheeled travel allied to performance in excess of that of any mass produced model and all but a handful of the hand built specials. Top speed varied from test to test but usually came out around 130 mph on those early models with some creeping closer to 135 and others pulling out around 125. Standing start quarter times were consistantly in the low 12's with a good one clocking 12·0 and average around 12·2 seconds.

The handling was acceptable for the fast tourer but no more. If the full performance was used on the road the rider could find that he had dialled up an exciting time and the weight made it a different proposition to the triples. With those you stood some chance of forcing the bike back to where you wanted it but the four was too heavy for tricks like that – it made the choice and forced the rider to go with it.

By the standards of the 1980s the Z1 handled poorly but in 1972 such matters were less advanced and the chassis did have to cope with a lot of power and weight. Thus it was struggling to a degree and the high wide bars were no help as at speed they forced the rider to pull on them to stay aboard. So for touring it was fine, for fast touring fine, for sports riding acceptable but for hard sporting rides needed much improved rear units, fork modifications and better tyres.

Not that there was any shortage of trick parts to fit after a year or two. Tuners soon grasped the potential of the big 4 and very quickly Z1s were being run in sprints and production racing. At first the motors were left standard but soon special cams, better ignition, big bore kits, racing pistons and the rest were on the market and boosting performance. The engine took it all without a murmur and it was only when the drag racers began to use superchargers that problems came. The crankshaft began to object to the power and abrupt clutch dumping by twisting so for quick use it was welded together at strategic points.

For normal street use most riders either settled for stock or just changed to better ignition coils and a 4 into 1 exhaust. In that form the engine would run and run. Even when tricked out with many of the hot parts the Kawasaki would still trundle on for tens of thousands of miles.

They ruled the drag strips in the USA and on the road could run away from the rest. Some of these street machines would run with all the quick parts under a stock exterior and this was often either ratty and tired looking or decked out with full touring gear from stem to stern. One such was capable of turning in an under 12 second quarter with near 120 mph terminal speed and broke many Honda hearts.

On the chassis side more work was needed to improve matters and for street use better bearings in the headstock and rear fork, European tyres and better rear units helped a good deal. For the track it was necessary to try to brace the frame so tubes would be welded into the area behind the headstock, fork damping would be modified and the engine mountings changed so all the fixings were a snug fit in both engine and frame.

The brakes worked well in the dry but less so when wet and suffered from lag as the pads desperately tried to sweep the water film from the disc. Slots and holes were then the preferred means of fixing the trouble and it was some years before Kawasaki led the way to the correct pad material that removed the problem. For competition there was the dual disc option and in many cases the calipers were moved behind the fork legs and the discs well thinned down to reduce the important unsprung weight.

The Z1 rolled into 1973 as 'King of the road' and was joined in January by the Z2 which was a smaller version for the Japanese market. The capacity was 746 cc and achieved by a slight reduction in bore size to 64 mm and a much shorter 58 mm stroke. Compression ratio was up a little at 9·0:1 and power a very respectable 69 bhp at 9000 rpm.

In just about every other way the Z2 copied

the Z1 down to the chain oil pump. The gearing was lowered by fitting a rear wheel sprocket with an extra 7 teeth and the quarter mile time was claimed to be 12·5 seconds.

Early in 1973 the four range was joined by a pair of police models, these being the Z1P and Z2P based on the stock machines but built to a police specification. In two years the larger machine had become the Police Special and was sold direct to USA precincts, mainly on the West Coast. Once a batch was sold a local dealer was appointed to handle service and spares and as a back-up Kawasaki established a police bike spares warehouse in Santa Ana.

The machine was based on the Z1 engine, frame, brakes and wheels but was fitted out from end to end with special features for police work. The exhaust was 4 into 2, crash bars were fitted front and rear while folding footboards and a special single seat ensured comfort despite long hours in the saddle. A rocking gear pedal was fitted and linked to the standard gearshift while a host of electrical items were added to a special wiring system. The screen was shatterproof and bullet resistant, and beside it went extra flashing blue lights.

In later years the big Kawasaki police bikes were to become even better known in their role with the California Highway Patrol through the medium of the TV programme 'CHiPs'. Ponch and John were the stars but the motorcycles were the theme showing how adaptable they could be whether on pursuit or threading through blocked traffic to sort out an incident.

Back in Japan at the end of 1973 a second test course was completed at the Akashi works and the four ran into 1974 as the Z1A. In England the importing franchise went briefly back to

All the big Kawasaki fours proclaimed their twin overhead camshafts by suitable markings on the outer engine covers, this is the Z1B from 1975

C. Itoh who were general Kawasaki agents in that country but early in the year Kawasaki Motors (UK) was formed with premises at first close to London Airport and later at Slough, a little further out. They had six machines to import and set out on a course new to the motorcycle trade in the seventies, sole brand agencies. With a restricted range of models to offer they were unable to cover all aspects of the market so altered their agreements to allow the dealer to stock other non-Japanese makes and followed the lines already proving successful in the USA.

Dealers received a massive sales and promotion guide that set out the house style among its many details and quickly the network built up and the model range began to expand. In five years it reached 30 machines, a five-fold increase, and the success of the solus policy was confirmed.

For the Z1A in 1974 the tank decor was changed to narrow stripes along the length and the colours were candy orange or candy yellow. In addition the black engine finish was dropped and the top half left in the natural alloy. A stop-light warning bulb was added, set in the rev-counter, and there were some improvements to ignition and carburettor areas.

Café racer models also began to appear prepared by some of the specialists and the best of these featured cockpit fairings, new seats and one piece tank cover, seat base and tail section in fibreglass. Special cast wheels, rearsets, clip-ons and special exhaust systems all complimented the ultra reliable motor to give both style and speed.

In August that year Kawasaki Motorcycle Canada was established which later became Canadian Kawasaki Motors and in November across the border in Nebraska a new plant was completed. This had manufacturing and assembly facilities and became the Kawasaki Motors Manufacturing Corpn. and was situated at Lincoln. By 1980 it could claim to be the largest motorcycle producer in the USA and one of the aids Kawasaki had was their own industrial robot, the Unimate.

1975 brought the Z1B and a number of changes including a sealed rear chain and the removal of the chain oil pump and its tank. This in turn brought to a halt the normal burnt oil finish of the left silencer pair that resulted from the pump. The marking was changed slightly and the colours became candy super blue or red. Internally a two-piece head gasket was adopted and during the year the primary drive was modified to cut down on the gear whine.

For the factory 1975 was also a good year with production starting at the Lincoln plant with a 400 cc 4-stroke twin. Two more subsidiaries were set up, the first being Kawasaki Motoren GmbH in West Germany and the second Kawasaki Motors Pty in Australia. At home in Akashi the technological engineering centre was completed and this consolidated the motorcycle design and test departments.

During the middle of 1975 two further police models were released as the KP900A and KP750A. These were much as the earlier Z series but their new nomenclature was reflected by the production model in 1976 when it became the Z900-A4. In this form power was down a touch thanks to smaller 26 mm carburettors but refinement was up and there were detail improvements. Noticeable ones were twin discs fitted as standard at the front and these were thinned down a good deal to reduce unsprung weight. The tank marking was changed a little and the colours were new, in diamond dark green or brown while the tank had a locking filler cap which used the same key as the ignition and seat lock. Less obvious changes were to the frame which benefited from heavier gauge tubing and other detail improvements, a lower battery mounting and raised gearing with two less teeth on the rear wheel sprocket.

Electrical changes included the 3 fuse system used by other models, an audible turn signal warning, 4 way hazard flashers and revised warn-

Right **Start of a trend, the 1976 Z900 LTD custom model built as a limited edition in a style copied by the other companies**

Below **English built special based on the Z1 and in the café racer style with Ace bars and rearsets**

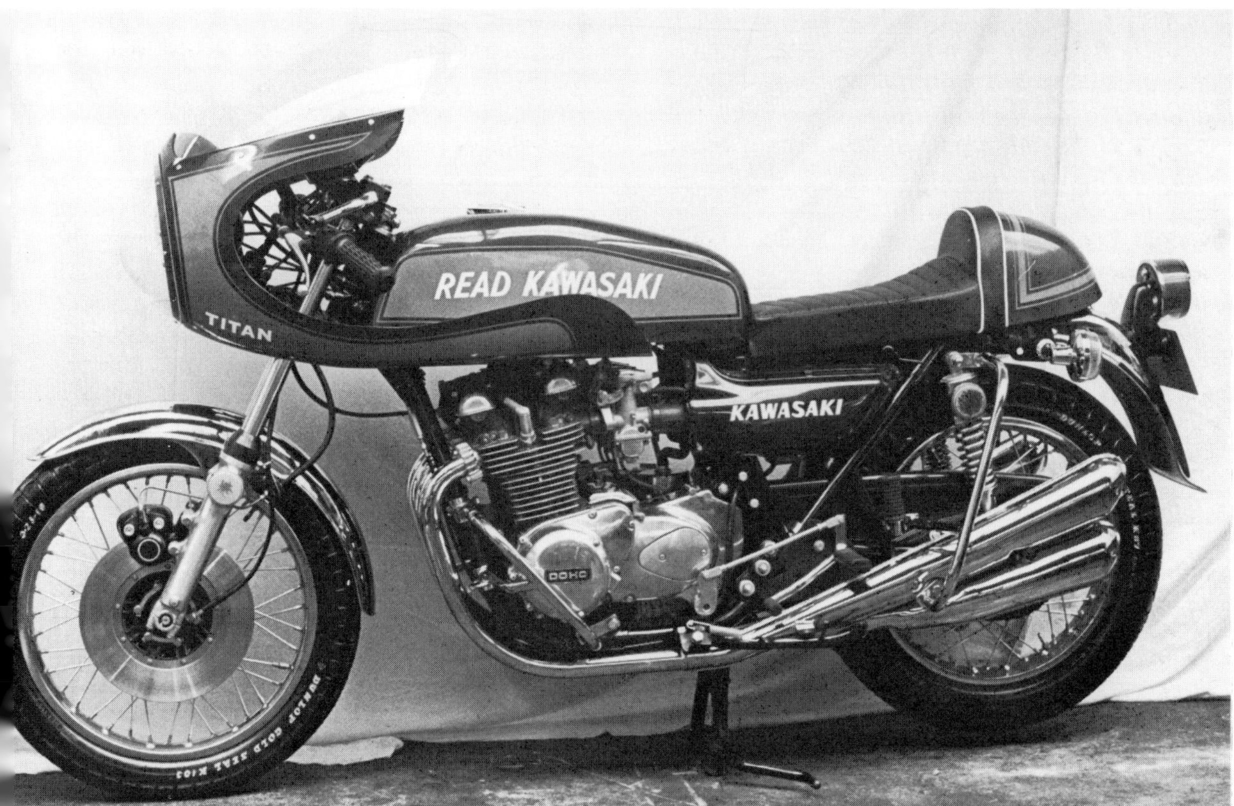

ing lights. These meant a new arrangement between the instruments with the ignition key low down flanked by the two turn lights and a column of lights above with, from the top, neutral, high beam, oil and stop bulb. The speedometer, with trip and total odometers, went on the left with the rev-counter, red-lined at 9000, on the right. The turn signal warning buzzer was thought by some authorities to be confusing to blind pedestrians at road crossings and the 4 way hazard unnecessary on a narrow motorcycle so both these features were dropped after a year or two.

1976 saw the debut of another version of the big Kawasaki and in its way it was as significant as any of their earlier models. It was the Z900-B1, better known as the Z900 LTD and was the first Japanese model built in the custom mould. LTD stood for 'Limited Edition' and it was followed by similar machines from all the other manufacturers until it became common practice for all the ranges to include custom versions.

Kawasaki launched the model with a further advantage for while the engine unit was built in Japan the machine was put together in the Nebraska factory so was able to carry a 'Made in USA' label. The motor and its transmission were stock 900 without change but fitted with a Jardine 4 into 2 exhaust that terminated in a shallow megaphone style silencer on each side.

The frame retained its rear suspension but with Mulholland units controlling its movement while standard forks went on to the front. Wheels were very different from stock being Morris cast aluminium with seven spokes and shod with Goodyear Eagle GT tyres. The front remained at 19 in. but the rear was a fat 16 in.

The brakes were discs all round with the dual front pair a slightly larger diameter than those on the stock 900 and lighter by dint of 2 mm less thickness. The calipers were mounted behind the fork legs on this model and this move worked well. At the rear a single disc was bolted to a new, smaller hub which retained the sprocket shock absorber of the drum brake version. The caliper was of the fixed type with two opposing pistons to move the brake pads and the assembly was mounted as an arm pivoted on the wheel spindle and restrained by a torque link acting in compression above the rear fork leg. The brake was operated by a small master cylinder linked by a push rod to the rear brake pedal and the original stop light switch was retained.

The mudguards were shortened and kept their chrome plating while the instrument pods were also given that finish. The headlight assembly mounting was altered and the fuel tank made

Right **Immaculate Rickman frame gave this Z1 engine a special style and excellent handling**

Far right **Custom special based on Z1 with cast wheels, rear disc, new tank and seat, windscreen, 4-into-1 exhaust and windtone horns**

slimmer with a reduced capacity. Very easy to spot was the new seat which was contoured to two levels in custom style with a reshaped grab rail behind it. The bars were pulled back and in and styling changes brought trimmer side covers and a chrome chainguard. They lost the centre stand which fell victim to the new exhaust system but the prop remained.

Colour of the tank, side covers and tailbox was classic red and Kawasaki built 2000 of them for the year. They sold immediately at a premium price and the only odd thing was that no more were built that year. The custom version of the big four was again a limited production the next year but from its first venture into the market came a whole stream of machines from all the firms.

At the end of 1976 the original Z1 came to its end. It was then stretched out to a litre and over the years joined by many brothers in touring, sports, cafe racer and custom styles. Later still they were joined by many smaller fours and the fabulous, enormous six.

By the late seventies the market was full of in-line fours but Kawasaki continued to lead from the front. As from the first Z1 they lived up to their signature—King of the road.

8 Extensive competition

Above **Hugh Evans urging his H1 out of Governor's Bridge, he was 5th in the 500 cc production race in 1972**

Top **Dave Simmonds with several 125 cc works twins in 1967**

Kawasaki's competition record runs back to the Meguro link and their success in 1957 at the historic Asama races. That year the old company took the 500 cc event with its overhead camshaft single so was among those whose roots sprang from those volcanic ashes. With the establishment of the Kawasaki name, they looked to the competition arena for a means to publicize it and the result was the success of the Red Tank 125 in the 1963 Japanese moto-cross championship.

From those early days, Kawasaki moved towards road racing for this gave them the maximum of press coverage and was to enable them to emphasize their dedication to performance. In later years they also went into trials and moto-cross as the off road sports became big business while their machines were used for most forms of two-wheeled competition.

The first Kawasaki appearance on the grand prix scene was in October 1965 at the Japanese meeting. They ran a number of 125 cc disc valve, water cooled, twins but these all retired and were none too competitive with the Suzuki twins and Honda 5s. In 1966 an improved model ran at the West German and on this occasion the machine ran much better. It was still in the same format with two water-cooled cylinders and disc valves while the exhausts came from the rear of the engine and a dry clutch on the right drove an eight-speed gearbox. Both mains and big ends were positively lubricated and the power unit went

Above **Dave in his championship year, 1969, with the Kawasaki motoring well**

Left **The works 125 with twin rear exhausts and fairing sides bulged out to clear the carburettors**

into a conventional chassis. This had telescopic fork front and pivoted fork rear suspension, a double sided drum front brake with single leading shoes on each side, drum rear brake and alloy wheel rims.

In the race it held 6th place until it retired on lap 6 and was ridden by Toshio Fujii who was due to race it in the 125 cc TT but sadly died following a practice crash. This reduced the factory interest in the class but they did appear at the Japanese meeting with their twins and a 125 cc four. In the event they used the twins and recruited two English riders, Christ Vincent, better known for his exploits with a BSA sidecar, and Dave Simmonds who had made a name in England with Itom and Tohatsu machines.

The factory decided to contest the 125 cc world championship for 1967 and chose Dave Simmonds to be their rider. Once set up, he was left much on his own to do battle with the Kawasaki's piston problems and full works teams from Suzuki and Yamaha. In addition he also had to cope with MZ, Bultaco, Montesa and private Hondas so had a hard year. Despite the difficulties he managed a 4th in the TT and a 3rd in Finland and also rode an A1R to 4th in the 250 cc TT and other placings.

Right **The works 500 cc triple in 1971 still with wire spoke wheels, drum brakes and narrow ribbed tyres**

Below **Christian Leon during the 1973 French GP 500 cc event in which he was 4th, twin discs now fitted at front**

The Japanese GP held at the end of the season was always important to the home firms and often saw the debut and trial in practice of some of their most advanced racing models. 1967 saw Kawasaki bring out a V4 of 125 cc much on the lines of the Yamaha. In the event they stuck with the twins and were rewarded with 3rd and 4th places.

1968 should have been better but Simmonds was off form due to a crash late the previous year and without his preparation skills, Kawasaki could achieve little. The racing versions of the 250 and 350 twins had the odd success and also ran at Daytona where a 250 was 7th in the 100 mile event.

If it had been a poor year there was compensation in 1969. Dave Simmonds had the 125 Kawasaki really on song and after missing the first championship round, won the West German by a narrow margin. He followed this with a 2nd in the French and then went to the Isle of Man for the TT. He won there and followed this by an incredible sequence in Holland, Belgium, Czechoslovakia, East Germany, Finland and Italy, winning every race. In the final round in Yugoslavia, he was second but this was academic for he had long since taken the world title.

Thus in that memorable year, Kawasaki won their first TT and titles for both man and machine. The new Mach III nearly made it two TTs for in the 500 cc class of the production race, Tony Dunnell was well ahead when he came adrift.

In 1970 it was less easy and the best Simmonds could do was 4th in the title chase with a single

Right **Mick Grant sails over Ballaugh Bridge on his way to winning the Senior TT for Kawasaki in 1975**

Below **Barry Ditchburn corners his triple in the North West 200**

Above **Daytona 1973 with Cliff Carr holding his 750 ahead of Don Castro on a 350 Yamaha. Cliff punctured when 3rd, Don finished 9th**

Left **French-Canadian Yvon DuHamel, a tough, hard rider who used the triple's power to the full**

win in Finland. This was compensated by the performance of the H1R, the first full 500 cc racer to be available for many years. Ginger Molloy got one and promptly finished 2nd to Agostini and his MV in the French. He was also 2nd in three more events and in the 500 cc world championship while Bill Smith took one to 3rd in the TT. Suddenly the 2-stroke was competitive in the most important racing class and from then on would move to a dominant position.

Molloy was also 7th at Daytona, an event Kawasaki never seemed to have the best of luck at although they had won the 100 miles in 1970. In that year they still lacked a 750 but this became available in 1971 and in that year Canadian Yvon DuHamel won for them at Talladega. In Europe Dave Simmonds struggled on with a diminishing supply of spares for the 125 but did manage to win the West German although relegated to the lower placings in other classics. He also took the 500 to its first championship win at the last classic of the year in Spain and he, and other riders, had some good placings during the year.

In 1971 Kawasaki also tried a new field of racing at the 24 hour Bol d'Or held at Le Mans and took the 500 cc class and 5th place overall. Out in the Far East Ken Araoka continued to win events such as the Philippine and Macau GPs just as he had taken classes at Singapore and Kuala Lumpur in the past.

1972 saw the last races of the 125 in Europe with a 3rd in Holland the best result for Dave Simmonds who died tragically in a caravan fire late in the year. The 500 found itself with more competition with MV running two machines most of the time and both Suzuki and Yamaha pushing it down the field. It did manage a number of useful placings including a third in the TT with rider Mick Grant, a prophetic event as it turned out.

DuHamel during a pit stop with pressure hose for fuel in, top pipe for air out and strong board for correct halt

17
KAWASAKI
17

The 750 had a much better year although Daytona was something of a disaster with the Kawasakis, managed by Bob Hansen, falling by the wayside. Paul Smart never really got going and pulled out after two laps, DuHamel seized after holding the lead and Gary Nixon had the gearbox go. Fortunately matters improved and DuHamel won at Talladega and Smart at Ontario in what was then the richest road race in the world. It netted him $30,400, or around £12,500 at the exchange rate then current.

The machine Smart used at Ontario had a frame built by Colin Seeley in England to improve the somewhat odd handling. At that time the American riders were none too concerned with this aspect while DuHamel was famous for his ability to ride anything fast regardless of how it behaved.

In Europe Kawasaki again won the 500 cc class in the Bol d'Or and in Australia the Castrol 6 hour race while Molloy won the Victorian TT. That same year also saw them reaping success off-road with Brad Lackey taking the AMA motocross championship. The machine he used was the F12MX and followed on the heels of earlier two-stroke singles, most of them finished in the characteristic Kawasaki lime green.

In 1973 the Green Meanie 750s continued to be successful and won at Laguna Seca and Ontario but had their seemingly inevitable upset at Daytona. In that race Art Baumann and DuHamel fell off together when in the lead because one hit some split oil and took the other off with him. The other two Kawasakis both stopped early on, one minus sparks and the other with a burnt piston. In Canada DuHamel won as did Molloy at Singapore but in many ways it was the exploits of the new Z1 that took the attention of press and public.

Kawasaki themselves set the ball rolling at Daytona in March with three machines, two near stock and the third worked on to show some of what could be done. Into that engine went a reground camshaft with more lift, gas-flowed ports, racing valve springs, different carburettors and a four-into-one exhaust system. This modified cylinder head sat on a stock engine and pushed out 105 bhp at 10,500 rpm. For the banked oval the machine was fitted with a fairing, H2R seat, Goodyear racing tyres, clip-ons, Koni rear units and heavy duty front springs. The rear chain was a Dense Lube self oiling type and the fuel tank had a quick filler valve set in its left side.

In this near standard form the Z1 lapped Daytona at 160·288 mph and recorded a top speed of 175 mph. With DuHamel riding it, 45 Ameri-

Right **The near standard Z1 with worked head, H2R seat and better carburettors which lapped Daytona at 160 mph**

Left **Australian Gregg Hansford well down to it on his triple**

can and worlds records for speed and endurance were taken but for the important 24 hours, two other machines were prepared.

These both had carefully assembled engines that had been ported and polished. The chassis used Koni rear dampers and to aid rider comfort clip-ons were fitted. The turn indicators were removed but otherwise the machines were standard. Two teams of four riders went into action running the engines between 7000 and 8000 rpm. Every 60 miles they refuelled and at every other stop changed riders. They ran for the 24 hours without any real hitch, each machine had a tyre change and one had a chain break. The centre stands tended to ground on the banking due to centrifugal force so their springs were reinforced with rubber bands but as with all successful, long distance runs, it was dull, boring and wearing.

At the end all the work was worthwhile for they had the new record having covered 2631·402 miles in the 24 hours, an average of 109·641 mph.

The Z1 went on that year to win the Australian 6 hour race and the Le Mans 1000 Km event while at the Bol d'Or it took 2nd, 4th and 5th places. In another run a stock machine complete with all fittings including the indicators covered 200 miles at an average of 130·434 mph. Even the standard bars were used but reversed to allow

DAYTONA
KAWASAKI
Kawasaki

Above **Olle Pettersson with the early motocross machine**

Left **End of the 24 hours record breaking at Daytona in 1973 when the machines averaged 109 and 104 mph for the full day**

the rider to get down to it and once in top gear, his feet perched on the pillion rests.

In other fields of racing the 500 was finding its days numbered but managed the occasional place and off-road Hansen was 4th in the 250 cc moto-cross world championship while Brad Lackey picked up a few points in the 500 cc class.

Kawasaki powered machines also ran in the 750 cc sidecar moto-cross class using the H2 engine which helped put them 4th in the table. The smooth triple certainly pushed out the power but lacked the punch the popular Norton twin had to get traction. The answer was to tune the crankshaft so all three cylinders fired together and the resulting thump dug down to grip.

1974 was the year Kawasaki went endurance racing with a vengeance using machines based on the Z1 engine in an Egli frame. Their top riding team was Georges Godier and Alain Genoud and the machine was purpose built for long distance events; tough, exceptionally easy to work on with numerous quickly detachable parts and

Above **Don Smith demonstrates the KT250 with the aid of a Beetle carrying Z1 stickers**

Top **Geoff Mayes testing the prototype KX380 with alloy rear fork and offset front spindle**

Right **Torleif Hansen in full flight in 1975**

NGK
Kawasaki

with the essentials tucked in so a fall damaged nothing that could not be replaced in seconds.

Godier and Genoud won at Barcelona, at Mettet and the Bol d'Or at Le Mans. In the 1000 Km at the same circuit a Kawasaki machine again won as did one at Oss in Holland. In England the Thruxton endurance race, run over 400 miles, was won by an H2R ridden by Barry Ditchburn and Kork Ballington which compensated for the lack of results with the triple in open races.

Kawasaki also won a production TT class in 1974 when Keith Martin took the *Motorcycle Mechanics* H1E to victory. His average was 93·85 mph which said a good deal about the potential of the Kawasaki and Keith's riding ability.

Off-road the Kawasakis went well enough for Jim Weinert to become the AMA motocross champion and T. Hansen to win two 250 cc GP events. So all told it was a good year for the firm and even at Daytona they managed a 3rd.

1975 was better, especially for the endurance racer, and the Godier and Genoud team won the title for the year based on the results of the 5 important races. They won the Bol d'Or, where Kawasakis were 2nd, 3rd and 5th, and were

Above **Nigel Birkett on his Kawasaki in a 1974 trial**

Right **Colin Dommett with his Kawasaki powered outfit in the 1975 British Experts which he won**

39
Kawasaki

placed at Thruxton and Mugello. Luc and Vial won the English event on the Kawasaki and were second at Montjuich which put them 4th in the table.

The works had new watercooled triples that year and ran in the 750 championship with some success. DuHamel won at Assen and Barry Ditchburn was placed in Sweden and at Silverstone. He and Mick Grant had been recruited to the team that year and Mick had a very good UK season for he won the Senior TT on the 500, broke Hailwood's long standing 1967 absolute TT lap record in the Open Classic and won the Superbike series in which Ditchburn was second.

It was the start of a four year association between Kawasaki and Mick Grant during which he established himself as a top factory rider and TT star. In that first year he and the others rode the 250 cc tandem twin that in later years was to take a whole string of titles, both as a 250 and also in enlarged 350 cc form.

In 1976 it was the turn of Gary Nixon on the 750 cc triple to make the news and he began at Daytona. On paper the green Kawasaki was overrun by yellow Yamahas with black stripes and for much of the race Roberts and Cecotto ran at the front. Then right at the end, Roberts' rear tyre went and Cecotto finished with the cords showing and rubber shredding from his tyre so one more lap would have stopped him to let Nixon through. It was the closest Kawasaki were to come to a Daytona win.

The second place gave Nixon a good start in the 750 cc championship but round two was at San Carlos in Venezuela and it both started and finished in chaos. Two legs were run and Cecotto won the first and Baker the second with Nixon second in both. Overall this gave the race to the Kawasaki rider but Baker claimed to have been

Pit stop for the famous Egli Kawasaki with Alain Genoud on the machine and Georges Godier standing, watching and waiting

67
MAHA
TOTAL
GENOUD
Kawasaki
GLI-KAWASAKI
68
SEGURA
KONI
MARCHAL
ER GENOUD
devil
MICHELI
MOTO
EGLI
TOTAL
devil

Kawasaki
Kawasaki
Kawasaki
MOTUL
2

Kawasaki
Hansford
MOTUL
Kawasaki
11

Far left above **DuHamel inside Stan Woods on the works Honda at the 1976 Bol d'Or where they were 3rd and 4th**

Left **Engine room of the watercooled triple**

Far left below **Special road racing four with reed valve induction. Stepped, in-line, layout with outer cylinders ahead of inner and not in a square as came later**

Below **One model racing was promoted by the Kawasaki KH400 series. This is Phil Hetherington who dominated the UK events in 1979**

Above **This insurance write-off brought Andy Pilgrim second place in the 1979 400 series at low cost. Box stock engines kept the racing close**

Right **The Hank Vink sprinter in 1977 with one engine and supercharger**

second in the first leg despite a brief pit stop. There was claim, counter-claim, lost lap charts and the matter dragged on to late in the year when the race and its results were deleted from the championship.

Meanwhile Baker won at Imola and Nixon missed Jarama as only at the last moment did the race become eligible. In Belgium he won and was placed in France but then Victor Palomo on a Yamaha began a run of success with wins in England, Holland and Germany where Nixon was 2nd.

When the points were added up, Palomo had 61 and Nixon 47 plus the 15 from San Carlos to make 62, hence the importance of the result to him. Sadly for Kawasaki and him, they were not counted so the title many thought to be his went elsewhere.

The endurance machines were unable to hold back a flood of Hondas that year but nearly upset them at the most important race of all, the Bol d'Or. In the end they had to be content with 2nd and 3rd but for a while had the winning Honda well worried.

So Kawasaki began to move away from their triples although the 750 took Grant to two Classic TT wins in 1977 and 1978. The 400 cc road triple was used to run a production machine series but this never reached the levels the later Yamaha ProAm races did.

The big four continued to run well in long distance events with a number of good placings but

no outright wins. What could be done with the basic material was once again demonstrated in 1979 when Graham Crosby rode the Moriwaki Kawasaki Formula 1 machine with straight bars in a manner that electrified the crowds and quickly brought him a Suzuki works contract.

In sprints and drag races many Kawasakis hit the headlines. The original H1 did well straight from the crate but in later days as many as three triple engines went into one machine to run 8 second times. The four was if anything more successful and one of the first to exploit it was Dutchman Henk Vink, Kawasaki's distributor in Holland. There were many, many more and they ran hard and fast.

The ultimate accolade came in 1978 when Don Vesco moved the motorcycle world speed record on to 318·598 mph. To do this he used a full streamliner with two turbocharged Kawasaki four engines fitted one behind the other and connected by two toothed belts, one on each side.

Back in Japan where it all started, the Kawasaki forerunner, Meguro, was still showing in competition in the late 1970s. The meetings were such as could only occur in that country for they were gambling matches with big money on the track and behind the scenes. Races were short and sharp, 6 laps of a 500 metre paved oval and such events had first been run in the 1920s.

In the hectic days in the late 1940s they revived and the money brought racketeers on a scale normally associated with Chicago and prohibition. It became a national scandle and was cleaned up but behind the facade deals still took place, big money was made and a visit into Tokyo bay wearing cement was not unheard of.

The rules and machines used were archaic as nothing built later than the 1950s was allowed so the days of the rather shady business were

Kawasaki
Lightning Bo

Far left **Twin engines of the record breaker ridden by Don Vesco to over 318 mph in 1978. A toothed belt went on each side of the engines**

Left below **The Vesco record breaker in flight**

Left **Ancient overhead camshaft Meguro single constructed to run on the Japanese ovals**

numbered as spares grew scarcer. The bikes were English Triumphs in the largest class with a few 650 cc overhead camshaft Meguro singles still running. In the smaller classes the Meguros were also to be seen along with Toyo and Kyokuto makes, all cast much in the European style of design of the 1940s. Hefty cam drive chambers ran up the right side of the single cylinder engines and the complete machines owed much to speedway. No brakes were fitted and only two speed gearboxes while frames were rigid and telescopic fork movement minimal. It was tough and exciting with frequent falls at high speeds.

So Kawasaki competition ran through many facets from the gambling ovals with historical machines, through the mist on the TT mountain, for 24 hours at Le Mans and down the drag strip for 9 short seconds. They ran in all sizes, won world titles, took records and lived up to that unspoken synonym for Kawasaki—performance.

Appendix

Specifications

Model	M50	MT1	GA0	GA1
Year from	**1967**	**1970**	**1969**	**1968**
Year to		**1975**		**1974**
No. cylinders	1	1	1	1
Bore (mm)	41	46	47	47
Stroke (mm)	37·8	44	51·8	51·8
Capacity (cc)	49·9	73	89·9	89·9
Compression ratio (to 1)	6·8	6·7	7·0	7·0
Induction	piston	piston	disc	disc
bhp	4·5	5·0 **1**	10·5	10·5
@ rpm	7000	6300 **1**	8000	8000
torque (Kg-m)	0·51	0·57	0.98	0·98
@ rpm	5000	5500	7000	7000
Starting system	elec, kick	kick	kick	kick
Oil system	petroil	pump	pump	pump
Port timing:				
Inlet opens			120	120
Inlet	62·5	63	55	55
Transfer	51·5	54·5	57·5	57·5
Exhaust	71·5	73	84·5	84·5
Ignition timing degree	25	21	20	20
Ignition timing (mm)	2·61	1·85	1·96	1·96
Primary drive gearing	14/55	17/57	21/74	21/74
Final drive gearing	13/40	13/33	14/39	14/39
Box gearing: top	1·15	1·05	1·0	1·0
Box gearing: 3rd			1·24	1·24
Box gearing: 2nd	1·53	1·53	1·71	1·71
Box gearing: 1st	2·91	2·91	2·92	2·92
O/A top gear ratio	13·9	8·94	9·82	9·82
No. gears	3	3	4	4
Fuel (l)	3·7	3·0	6·5 **2**	6·5 **3**
Engine oil (l)		0·9	1·2	1·2
Box oil (l)	0·75	1·0	0·7	0·7
Front fork/leg (cc)			130	130

Model	M50	MT1	GA0	GA1
Year from	**1967**	**1970**	**1969**	**1968**
Year to		**1975**		**1974**
Front tyre	2·25 × 17	3·50 × 8	2·50 × 18	2·50 × 18
Rear tyre	2·25 × 17	3·50 × 8	2·50 × 18	2·50 × 18
Front brake	drum	105 drum	drum	110 × 30
Rear brake	drum	105 drum	drum	110 × 30
Front suspension	leading link	teles	teles	teles
Rear suspension	s/a	s/a	s/a	s/a
Ignition system	magneto	magneto	magneto	magneto
Wheelbase (in.)	45·5	38·0	45·3	45·3
Ground clear. (in.)	4·9	4·5 **4**	5·9	5·9
Width (in.)	25·4	23·6	29·1	29·1
Length (in.)	72	53·1	71·3	71·3
Dry weight (lb)	154	121	174	174

1 1972—4·2/6500 **2** GA0-A—8·6 **3** 1971—8·6 **4** 1974—6·1

Model	GA2	GA3	GA4	G3TR
Year from	**1968**	**1968**	**1969**	**1968**
Year to	**1974**	**1970**	**1970**	**1970**
No. cylinders	1	1	1	1
Bore (mm)	47	47	47	47
Stroke (mm)	51·8	51·8	51·8	51·8
Capacity (cc)	89·9	89·9	89·9	89·9
Compression ratio (to 1)	7·0	7·0	7·0	7·0
Induction	disc	disc	disc	disc
bhp	10·5	10·5	10·5	10·5
@ rpm	8000	8000	8000	8000
torque (Kg-m)	0·98	0·98	0·98	0·98
@ rpm	7000	7000	7000	7000
Starting system	kick	kick	kick	kick
Oil system	pump	pump	pump	pump
Port timing:				
Inlet opens	120	120	120	120
Inlet	55	55	55	55
Transfer	57·5	57·5	57·5	57·5
Exhaust	84·5	84·5	84·5	84·5
Ignition timing degree	20	20	20	20
Ignition timing (mm)	1·96	1·96	1·96	1·96
Primary drive gearing	21/74	21/74	21/74	21/74
Final drive gearing	14/36	14/39	14/42	14/39
Box gearing: top	0·96	0·96	0·96	0·96
Box gearing: 4th	1·09	1·09	1·09	1·09
Box gearing: 3rd	1·30	1·30	1·30	1·30
Box gearing: 2nd	1·76	1·76	1·76	1·76
Box gearing: 1st	2·92	2·92	2·92	2·92
O/A top gear ratio	8·70	9·42	10·15	9·42
No. gears	5	5	5	5

Model	GA2	GA3	GA4	G3TR
Year from	**1968**	**1968**	**1969**	**1968**
Year to	**1974**	**1970**	**1970**	**1970**
Fuel (l)	6·5 **1**	8·6	9·5	8·6
Engine oil (l)	1·2	1·2	1·2	1·2
Box oil (l)	0·7	0·7	0·7	0·7
Front fork/leg (cc)	130	130	170	130
Front tyre	2·50 × 18	2·75 × 18	2·75 × 18	2·75 × 18
Rear tyre	2·50 × 18	2·75 × 18	3·00 × 18	2·75 × 18
Front brake	110 × 30	drum	drum	110 × 30
Rear brake	110 × 30	drum	drum	110 × 30
Front suspension	teles	teles	teles	teles
Rear suspension	s/a	s/a	s/a	s/a
Ignition system	magneto	magneto	magneto	magneto
Wheelbase (in.)	45·3	45·3	49·6	45·3
Ground clear. (in.)	5·9	6·7	9·1	6·3
Width (in.)	29·1	33·1	33·1	33·1
Length (in.)	71·3	72·0	75·8	72·0
Dry weight (lb)	174	180	187	178

1 1971—8·6

Model	MC1	MC1M	G2S	G2T
Year from	**1973**	**1973**	**1973**	**1973**
Year to	**1975**	**1975**	**1974**	**1976**
No. cylinders	1	1	1	1
Bore (mm)	47	47	47	47
Stroke (mm)	51·8	51·8	51·8	51·8
Capacity (cc)	89·9	89·9	89·9	89·9
Compression ratio (to 1)	6·8	6·8	7·0	7·0
Induction	disc	disc	disc	disc
bhp	6·6	6·6	10	10
@ rpm	6500	6500	7500	7500
torque (Kg-m)	0·81	0·81	0·98	0·98
@ rpm	5500	5500	7000	7000
Starting system	kick	kick	kick	kick
Oil system	pump	pump	pump	pump
Port timing:				
Inlet opens	120	120	120	120
Inlet	55	55	55	55
Transfer	54·9	54·9	57·5	57·5
Exhaust	75	75	83	83
Ignition timing degree	20	20	20	20
Ignition timing (mm)	1·96	1·96	1·96	1·96
Primary drive gearing	21/74	21/74	21/74	21/74
Final drive gearing	14/36	14/36	14/40	14/37 **1**
Box gearing: top	0·96	0·96	1·00	0·96
Box gearing: 4th	1·09	1·09		1·09
Box gearing: 3rd	1·30	1·30	1·24	1·30

Model	MC1	MC1M	G2S	G2T
Year from	**1973**	**1973**	**1973**	**1973**
Year to	**1975**	**1975**	**1974**	**1976**
Box gearing: 2nd	1·76	1·76	1·71	1·76
Box gearing: 1st	2·92	2·92	2·92	2·92
O/A top gear ratio	8·70	8·70	10·07	8·94 **2**
No. gears	5	5	4	5
Fuel (l)	6·0	6·0	8·6	8·6
Engine oil (l)	1·0	1·0	1·2	1·2
Box oil (l)	0·6	0·6	0·6	0·6
Front fork/leg (cc)	92	92	130	130
Front tyre	2·50 × 16	2·50 × 16	2·50 × 18	2·50 × 18
Rear tyre	2·75 × 14 **3**	2·75 × 14	2·50 × 18	2·50 × 18
Front brake	110 × 30	110 × 30	110 × 30	110 × 30
Rear brake	110 × 30	110 × 30	110 × 30	110 × 30
Front suspension	teles	teles	teles	teles
Rear suspension	s/a	s/a	s/a	s/a
Ignition system	magneto	magneto	magneto	magneto
Wheelbase (in.)	43·3	43·3	45·3	45·3
Ground clear. (in.)	6·3	6·3	5·9	5·9
Width (in.)	30·1	30·1	29·1	29·1
Length (in.)	68·1	65·6	71·3	71·3
Dry weight (lb)	165	150	181	181

1 1976—14/36 **2** 1976—8·70 **3** 1975—3·00 × 14

Model	G6	G8S	G8T	G3SS
Year from	**1972**	**1972**	**1972**	**1968**
Year to	**1974**	**1973**	**1973**	**1974**
No. cylinders	1	1	1	1
Bore (mm)	47	47	47	47
Stroke (mm)	51·8	51·8	51·8	51·8
Capacity (cc)	89·9	89·9	89·9	89·9
Compression ratio (to 1)	7·0	7·0	7·0	7·0
Induction	disc	disc	disc	disc
bhp	10	10	10	10·5 **1**
@ rpm	8000	8000	8000	8000 **1**
torque (Kg-m)	0·94	0·94	0·94	0·98
@ rpm	7500	7500	7500	7000
Starting system	kick	kick	kick	kick
Oil system	pump	pump	pump	pump
Port timing:				
Inlet opens	120	120	120	120
Inlet	55	55	55	55
Transfer	57·5	57·5	57·5	57·5
Exhaust	83	83	83	84·5 **2**
Ignition timing degree	20	20	20	20
Ignition timing (mm)	1·96	1·96	1·96	1·96
Primary drive gearing	21/74	21/74	21/74	21/74

Model	G6	G8S	G8T	G3SS
Year from	**1972**	**1972**	**1972**	**1968**
Year to	**1974**	**1973**	**1973**	**1974**
Final drive gearing	15/42	14/40	14/37	14/37
Box gearing: top	0·96	1·00	0·96	0·96
Box gearing: 4th	1·09		1·09	1·09
Box gearing: 3rd	1·30	1·24	1·30	1·30
Box gearing: 2nd	1·76	1·71	1·76	1·76
Box gearing: 1st	2·92	2·92	2·92	2·92
O/A top gear ratio	9·47	10·07	8·94	8·94
No. gears	5	4	5	5
Fuel (l)	8·0	10·0	10·0	8·6 **3**
Engine oil (l)	1·1	1·4	1·4	1·2 **4**
Box oil (l)	0·6	0·6	0·6	0·7
Front fork/leg (cc)	162	140	140	130
Front tyre	2·75 × 19	2·50 × 18	2·50 × 18	2·75 × 18 **5**
Rear tyre	3·00 × 18	2·50 × 18	2·50 × 18	2·75 × 18
Front brake	110 × 30	130 drum	130 drum	110 × 30
Rear brake	110 × 30	110 × 30	110 × 30	110 × 30
Front suspension	teles	teles	teles	teles
Rear suspension	s/a	s/a	s/a	s/a
Ignition system	magneto	magneto	magneto	magneto
Wheelbase (in.)	49·8	48·2	48·2	45·3
Ground clear. (in.)	9·6	5·9	6·1	6·3 **6**
Width (in.)	33·9	31·5	31·5	33·1
Length (in.)	78·0	75·0	76·6	72·0 **7**
Dry weight (lb)	201	196	196	178

1 1973—10/7500 **2** 1974—83 **3** 1974—8 **4** 1974—1·5 **5** 1974—2·50 × 18 **6** 1974—5·9 **7** 1974—71·7

Model	G3SSE	G3TRA	G4TR	GA5
Year from	**1975**	**1971**	**1969**	**1970**
Year to			**1975**	**1974**
No. cylinders	1	1	1	1
Bore (mm)	49·5	49·5	49·5	49·5
Stroke (mm)	51·8	51·8	51·8	51·8
Capacity (cc)	99·7	99·7	99·7	99·7
Compression ratio (to 1)	7·0	7·0	7·0	7·0
Induction	disc	disc	disc	disc
bhp	10·5	11·5	11·5 **1**	11·5
@ rpm	7500	8000	8000 **1**	8000
torque (Kg-m)	1·0	1·1	1·12 **2**	1·1
@ rpm	7000	7000	7000	7000
Starting system	kick	kick	kick	kick
Oil system	pump	pump	pump	pump
Port timing:				
Inlet opens	120	120	120	120
Inlet	55	55	55	55

Model	G3SSE	G3TRA	G4TR	GA5
Year from	**1975**	**1971**	**1969**	**1970**
Year to			**1975**	**1974**
Transfer	58·5	57·5	57·5 **3**	57·5
Exhaust	84·3	84·5	84·5 **4**	84·5
Ignition timing degree	20	20	20	20
Ignition timing (mm)	1·96	1·96	1·96	1·96
Primary drive gearing	21/74	21/74	21/74	21/74
Final drive gearing	14/37	14/42	15/42	14/36
Box gearing: top	0·96	0·96	0·96	0·96
Box gearing: 4th	1·09	1·09	1·09	1·09
Box gearing: 3rd	1·30	1·30	1·30	1·30
Box gearing: 2nd	1·76	1·76	1·76	1·76
Box gearing: 1st	2·92	2·92	2·92	2·92
O/A top gear ratio	8·94	10·15	9·47 **5**	8·70
No. gears	5	5	5	5
Fuel (l)	8·0	8·6	9·5 **6**	8·6
Engine oil (l)	1·5	1·2	1·2 **7**	1·2
Box oil (l)	0·6	0·7	0·7 **8**	0·7 **9**
Front fork/leg (cc)	130	130	170 **10**	130
Front tyre	2·50 × 18 **11**	2·75 × 18	3·00 × 18	2·75 × 18 **12**
Rear tyre	2·75 × 18 **13**	2·75 × 18	3·00 × 18	2·75 × 18
Front brake	110 × 30	110 × 30	110 × 30	110 × 30
Rear brake	110 × 30	110 × 30	110 × 30	110 × 30
Front suspension	teles	teles	teles	teles
Rear suspension	s/a	s/a	s/a	s/a
Ignition system	magneto	magneto	magneto	magneto
Wheelbase (in.)	45·3	45·3	50·0	45·3
Ground clear. (in.)	5·9	6·3	9·8	6·3
Width (in.)	33·1	33·1	33·1	33·1
Length (in.)	72·2	72·0	77·6	72·0
Dry weight (lb)	187	183	198 **14**	174

1 1973—11/7500 **2** 1973—1·1 **3** 1974—58·6 **4** 1974—84·3 **5** dual range—low 17·5 **6** 1973—8·3 **7** 1973—1·6 **8** 1973—0·6 **9** 1971—0·6 **10** 1973—162 **11** late 1975—2·75 × 18 **12** 1971—2·50 × 18 **13** late 1975—3·00 × 18 **14** 1974—209

Model	GA1	G5	G7S	G7T
Year from	**1972**	**1971**	**1973**	**1972**
Year to	**1974**	**1975**	**1975**	**1976**
No. cylinders	1	1	1	1
Bore (mm)	49·5	49·5	49·5	49·5
Stroke (mm)	51·8	51·8	51·8	51·8
Capacity (cc)	99·7	99·7	99·7	99·7
Compression ratio (to 1)	7·0	7·0	7·0	7·0
Induction	disc	disc	disc	disc
bhp	11·5	11·0	11·5	11·5
@ rpm	8000	7500	8000	8000
torque (Kg-m)	1·1	1·1	1·07	1·07

Model	GA1	G5	G7S	G7T
Year from	**1972**	**1971**	**1973**	**1972**
Year to	**1974**	**1975**	**1975**	**1976**
@ rpm	7000	7000	7000	7000
Starting system	kick	kick	kick	kick
Oil system	pump	pump	pump	pump
Port timing:				
Inlet opens	120	120	120	120
Inlet	55	55	55	55
Transfer	57·5	57·5 **1**	58·6	58·6
Exhaust	84·5	84·5 **2**	84·3	84·3
Ignition timing degree	20	20	20	20
Ignition timing (mm)	1·96	1·96	1·96	1·96
Primary drive gearing	21/74	21/74	21/74	21/74
Final drive gearing	13/42	15/42	14/40	14/37
Box gearing: top	1·00	0·96	1·00	0·96
Box gearing: 4th		1·09		1·09
Box gearing: 3rd	1·24	1·30	1·24	1·30
Box gearing: 2nd	1·71	1·76	1·71	1·76
Box gearing: 1st	2·92	2·92	2·92	2·92
O/A top gear ratio	11·38	9·47	10·07	8·94
No. gears	4	5	4	5
Fuel (l)	8·6	8·0	10·0	10·0
Engine oil (l)	1·2	1·2	1·4	1·4
Box oil (l)	0·7 **3**	0·7 **3**	0·6	0·6
Front fork/leg (cc)	130	162	140	140
Front tyre	2·50 × 18	2·75 × 18 **4**	2·50 × 18	2·50 × 18
Rear tyre	2·50 × 18	3·00 × 18	2·75 × 18	2·75 × 18
Front brake	110 × 30	110 × 30	130 drum	130 drum
Rear brake	110 × 30	110 × 30	110 × 30	110 × 30
Front suspension	teles	teles	teles	teles
Rear suspension	s/a	s/a	s/a	s/a
Ignition system	magneto	magneto	magneto	magneto
Wheelbase (in.)	45·3	49·6	48·2	48·2
Ground clear. (in.)	5·9	9·4	6·3	6·3
Width (in.)	29·1	33·9	31·5	31·5
Length (in.)	71·3	78·0	73·6	73·6
Dry weight (lb)	174	195	196	196

1 1974—58·6 **2** 1974—84·3 **3** 1973—0·6 **4** 1973—2·75 × 19

Model	G3T	G31M	B1L	F6
Year from	**1974**	**1969**	**1965**	**1970**
Year to	**1976**	**1971**	**1976**	**1973**
No. cylinders	1	1	1	1
Bore (mm)	49·5	49·5	55	52
Stroke (mm)	51·8	51·8	52·5	58·8
Capacity (cc)	99·7	99·7	124·7	124·9
Compression ratio (to 1)	7·0	7·8	6·4	7·2

Model	G3T	G31M	B1L	F6
Year from	**1974**	**1969**	**1965**	**1970**
Year to	**1976**	**1971**	**1976**	**1973**
Induction	disc	disc	disc	disc
bhp	10·5	17·5	12	17·5 **1**
@ rpm	7500	11000	6500	7500
torque (Kg-m)	1·0	1·13	1·35	1·4 **2**
@ rpm	7000	10500	5000	7000
Starting system	kick	kick	elec, kick	kick
Oil system	pump	mix	pump	pump
Port timing:				
Inlet opens	120	140	110	115
Inlet	55	70	45	55
Transfer	58·6	62	57·5	57·5
Exhaust	84·3	93	79·5	87
Ignition timing degree	20	23	20	23
Ignition timing (mm)	1·96		1·93	2·94
Primary drive gearing	21/74	21/74	21/68	24/75
Final drive gearing	14/37	14/50	15/42	14/55 **3**
Box gearing: top	0·96	0·96	0·90	0·72 **4**
Box gearing: 4th	1·09	1·09		0·91 **4**
Box gearing: 3rd	1·30	1·30	1·20	1·20 **4**
Box gearing: 2nd	1·76	1·61	1·62	1·75
Box gearing: 1st	2·92	2·36	2·67	2·67
O/A top gear ratio	8·94	12·08	8·16	8·84 **5**
No. gears	5	5	4	5
Fuel (l)	8·0		8·5	9·7 **6**
Engine oil (l)	1·5		1·8	1·6 **7**
Box oil (l)	0·6	0·6	0·9	0·7
Front fork/leg (cc)	130	115	175	152
Front tyre	2·50 × 18	3·25 × 18	3·00 × 16	3·00 × 18
Rear tyre	2·75 × 18	3·25 × 18	3·00 × 16	3·25 × 18
Front brake	110 × 30	130 × 30	150 × 28	130 × 28
Rear brake	110 × 30	130 × 30	150 × 28	130 × 28
Front suspension	teles	teles	teles	teles
Rear suspension	s/a	s/a	s/a	s/a
Ignition system	magneto	magneto	coil	magneto
Wheelbase (in.)	45·3	51·0	49·2	55·7 **8**
Ground clear. (in.)	5·9	10·2	5·3	9·6
Width (in.)	28·9	33·1	31·1 **9**	33·5
Length (in.)	73·2	76·4	77·4 **10**	78·7 **11**
Dry weight (lb)	187	178	257	231

1 1973—14·5 **2** 1973—1·43 **3** Japan only—14/46 **4** Japan only—0·96, 1·10, 1·32 **5** Japan only—9·86
6 1972 only—9·0 **7** 1973—1·5 **8** 1973—51·8 **9** 1974—30·9 **10** 1973 only—74·8 **11** 1972 only—74·8

Model	MB1	F7	SG	F8
Year from	**1969**	**1970**	**1964**	**1970**
Year to	**1971**	**1975**	**1969**	**1972**
No. cylinders	1	1	1	1
Bore (mm)	60	61·5	66	68
Stroke (mm)	47	58·8	72·6	68
Capacity (cc)	133	174·7	248	247
Compression ratio (to 1)	6·4	7·1 **1**	8·7	6·8
Valve type/Induction	SV	disc	ohv	disc
bhp	3·4	21·5 **2**	18	23·5
@rpm	4200	7500	7000	6800
torque (Kg-m)	0·62	2·12 **3**	2·0	2·64
@ rpm	3000	7000	5500	6000
Starting system	pull	kick	elec, kick	kick
Oil system	splash	pump	wet sump	pump
Valve/port timing:				
Inlet opens BTDC	62	115	15	110
Inlet closes ABDC	92	55	80	50
Transfer/Exhaust opens BBDC	97	55·5	80	59
Exhaust closes ATDC	57	82	15	83
Tappets, inlet (mm)	0·1/0·34		0·2	
Tappets, exhaust (mm)	0·1/0·34		0·2	
Ignition timing degree	23	23	5–31	20
Ignition timing (mm)	2·4	2·94		2·59
Primary drive gearing	15/30	24/75	16/45	24/73
Final drive gearing	15/72	14/50	15/37	14/45 **4**
Box gearing: top		0·72	1·0	0·71 **5**
Box gearing: 4th		0·91		0·90
Box gearing: 3rd		1·20	1·43	1·17
Box gearing: 2nd		1·75	2·04	1·71
Box gearing: 1st		2·67	2·98	2·45
O/A top gear ratio	9·6	8·04	6·94	6·94 **6**
No. gears	1	5	4	5
Fuel (l)	2·0	9·0 **7**	12	12·5
Engine oil (l)		1·5	2·0	1·6
Box oil (l)	0·5	0·7		1·2
Front fork/leg (cc)		115	200	175
Front tyre	3·25 × 8	3·00 × 19	3·00 × 18 **8**	3·25 × 19
Rear tyre	3·25 × 8	3·50 × 18	3·25 × 18 **9**	4·00 × 18
Front brake	nil	130 × 28	drum	150 × 28
Rear brake	drum	130 × 28	drum	150 × 28
Front suspension	teles	teles	teles	teles
Rear suspension	rigid	s/a	s/a	s/a
Ignition system	magneto	CDI	coil	magneto
Wheelbase (in.)	37·4	52·0	53·5	55·1
Ground clear. (in.)	5·5	9·8	5·3	8·3
Width (in.)	25·0	33·5	32·7	32·3
Length (in.)	52·0	80·3	80·7	82·3

Model	**MB1**	**F7**	**SG**	**F8**
Year from	**1969**	**1970**	**1964**	**1970**
Year to	**1971**	**1975**	**1969**	**1972**
Dry weight (lb)	93	233 **10**	363	270

1 1973—7·0 **2** 1972—18 **3** 1972—1·8 **4** Japan only—14/37 **5** Japan only—0·95, 1·09, 1·26, 1·60, 2·45
6 Japan only—7·64 **7** 1972—9·7 **8** size for SGT; SG—2·75 × 18 **9** size for SGT; SG—3·00 × 18 **10** 1973—239

Model	**F11**	**F81M**	**F5**	**F9**
Year from	**1971**	**1970**	**1969**	**1971**
Year to	**1975**	**1971**	**1971**	**1975**
No. cylinders	1	1	1	1
Bore (mm)	68	68	80·5	80·5
Stroke (mm)	68	68	68	68
Capacity (cc)	247	247	346	346
Compression ratio (to 1)	7·0 **1**	7·5	6·8	7·0
Induction	piston	disc	disc	disc
bhp	22	27	33	33 **2**
@ rpm	6500	6750	6500	6500
torque (Kg-m)	2·6	3·12	3·9	3·9 **3**
@ rpm	6000	5750	5000	5500
Starting system	kick	kick	kick	kick
Oil system	pump	mix	pump	pump
Port timing:				
Inlet opens		130	110	120
Inlet	71	65	50	60
Transfer	52	59	57	57
Exhaust	82	87·7	82	82
Ignition timing degree	20	19	23	23
Ignition timing (mm)	2·56		3·41	3·41
Primary drive gearing	24/72	24/73	24/73	24/73
Final drive gearing	13/43 **4**	14/45	14/41 **5**	14/41
Box gearing: top	0·75	0·95	0·71	0·71
Box gearing: 4th	0·91	1·09	0·90	0·90
Box gearing: 3rd	1·15 **6**	1·26	1·17	1·17
Box gearing: 2nd	1·63 **6**	1·60	1·71	1·71
Box gearing: 1st	2·5 **6**	2·45	2·45	2·45
O/A top gear ratio	7·44 **7**	9·29	6·32 **8**	6·32
No. gears	5	5	5	5
Fuel (l)	9·5	12·5	12·5	12·4 **9**
Engine oil (l)	1·4		1·6	1·6
Box oil (l)	1·2	1·0	1·2	1·2
Front fork/leg (cc)	170	175	175	175
Front tyre	3·00 × 21	3·00 × 21	3·00 × 21	3·00 × 21
Rear tyre	4·00 × 18	4·00 × 18	4·00 × 18	4·00 × 18
Front brake	150 × 28	150 × 28	150 × 28	150 × 28
Rear brake	150 × 28	150 × 28	150 × 28	150 × 28
Front suspension	teles	teles	teles	teles
Rear suspension	s/a	s/a	s/a	s/a

Model	F11	F81M	F5	F9
Year from	**1971**	**1970**	**1969**	**1971**
Year to	**1975**	**1971**	**1971**	**1975**
Ignition system	magneto	magneto	CDI	CDI
Wheelbase (in.)	54·9 **10**	55·1	55·1	54·3 **11**
Ground clear. (in.)	10·2 **12**	9·1	9·1	8·5 **13**
Width (in.)	32·3 **14**	35·4	32·3	33·5 **15**
Length (in.)	83·9 **16**	83·1	82·3	81·7 **17**
Dry weight (lb)	264	238	280	265 **18**

1 1974—6·4 **2** 1973—28 **3** 1973—3·3 **4** 1973—13/44 **5** 1971—14/45
6 Japan only and 1973 on—1·10, 1·47, 2·23 **7** 1973—7·62 **8** 1971—6·94 **9** 1974—11·0
10 1975—54.6 **11** 1974—55·1 **12** 1975—9·8 **13** 1974—9·1 **14** 1973—32·7 **15** 1974—33·7
16 1975—84·6 **17** 1974—82·3 **18** 1974—291

Model	F12MX	A1	A1SS	A1R
Year from	**1973**	**1966**	**1967**	**1967**
Year to		**1971**	**1971**	**1968**
No. cylinders	1	2	2	2
Bore (mm)	86	53	53	53
Stroke (mm)	76	56	56	56
Capacity (cc)	441	247	247	247
Compression ratio (to 1)	6·5	7·0	7·0	8·0
Induction	piston	disc	disc	disc
bhp	38	31	31	40
@ rpm	5500	8000	8000	9500
torque (Kg-m)	5·1	2·92	2·92	3·00
@ rpm	5000	7500	7500	8500
Starting system	kick	kick	kick	push
Oil system	mix	pump	pump	pump & mix
Port timing:				
Inlet opens		112	112	130
Inlet	72	65	65	70
Transfer	55·5	61 **1**	61 **1**	62
Exhaust	88	91 **2**	91 **2**	94·5
Ignition timing degree	25	23 **3**	23 **3**	23
Ignition timing (mm)	4·48	2·97 **4**	2·97 **4**	2·97
Primary drive gearing	23/58	15/51	15/51	17/57
Final drive gearing	15/43	15/37	15/39	16/29
Box gearing: top	0·94	0·78	0·78	0·89
Box gearing: 4th	1·12	0·92	0·92	1·00
Box gearing: 3rd	1·40	1·13	1·13	1·18
Box gearing: 2nd	2·00	1·53	1·53	1·47
Box gearing: 1st	2·89	2·50	2·50	2·06
O/A top gear ratio	6·80	6·54	6·90	5·41
No. gears	5	5	5	5
Fuel (l)	7·5	13·5	13·5	20
Engine oil (l)		2·2	2·2	1·0
Box oil (l)	0·95	1·2	1·2	1·2

Model	F12MX	A1	A1SS	A1R
Year from	**1973**	**1966**	**1967**	**1967**
Year to		**1971**	**1971**	**1968**
Front fork/leg (cc)	180	200	200	200
Front tyre	3·00 × 21	3·00 × 18	3·00 × 18	2·75 × 18
Rear tyre	4·00 × 18	3·25 × 18	3·25 × 18 **5**	3·00 × 18
Front brake	130 × 28	180 × 30	180 × 30	200 × 20(2)
Rear brake	150 × 28	180 × 30	180 × 30	180 × 36
Front suspension	telex	teles	teles	teles
Rear suspension	s/a	s/a	s/a	s/a
Ignition system	CDI	coil **6**	coil **6**	magneto
Wheelbase (in.)	55·5	51·0 **7**	51·0 **7**	51·0
Ground clear. (in.)	7·7	6·7 **8**	6·7	4·9
Width (in.)	34·4	32·7 **9**	32·7	22·8
Length (in.)	81·0	78·3	78·3	75·4
Dry weight (lb)	220	319	323	240

1 late—58 **2** late—89 **3** 25 for CDI system **4** 3·29 for CDI **5** late—3·50 × 18 **6** CDI for USA models from 1969
7 late—51·2 **8** late—6·5 **9** late—31·9

Model	A7	A7SS	A7R	S1 10
Year from	**1967**	**1967**	**1968**	**1971**
Year to	**1971**	**1971**		**1980**
No. cylinders	2	2	2	3
Bore (mm)	62	62	63	45
Stroke (mm)	56	56	56	52·3
Capacity (cc)	338	338	349	249·5
Compression ratio (to 1)	7·0	7·0	7·7	7·3 **1**
Induction	disc	disc	disc	piston
bhp	42	42	53	32 **2**
@ rpm	8000	8000	9500	8000 **2**
torque (Kg-m)	3·99	3·99	4·04	3·0 **3**
@ rpm	7000	7000	9500	7000
Starting system	kick	kick	push	kick
Oil system	pump	pump	pump & mix	pump
Port timing:				
Inlet opens	115 **4**	115 **4**	130	
Inlet	68 **5**	68 **5**	70	76·5
Transfer	60	60	63	60
Exhaust	91	91	98·5	83
Ignition timing degree	23 **6**	23 **6**	27	23
Ignition timing (mm)	2·97 **7**	2·97 **7**		2·6
Primary drive gearing	15/51	15/51	17/57	27/60
Final drive gearing	15/36	15/36	16/29	14/46 **8**
Box gearing: top	0·78	0·78	0·89	0·96
Box gearing: 4th	0·92	0·92	1·00	1·12
Box gearing: 3rd	1·13	1·13	1·18	1·35
Box gearing: 2nd	1·53	1·53	1·47	1·79
Box gearing: 1st	2·50	2·50	2·06	2·86

Model	A7	A7SS	A7R	S1 10
Year from	**1967**	**1967**	**1968**	**1971**
Year to	**1971**	**1971**		**1980**
O/A top gear ratio	6·36	6·36	5·41	7·01 **9**
No. gears	5	5	5	5
Fuel (l)	13·5	13·5	20	14 **11**
Engine oil (l)	2·2	2·2	1·0	1·5
Box oil (l)	1·2	1·2	1·2	1·1
Front fork/leg (cc)	200	200	220	210
Front tyre	3·25 × 18	3·25 × 18	2·75 × 18	3·00 × 18 **12**
Rear tyre	3·50 × 18	3·50 × 18	3·00 × 18	3·25 × 18 **13**
Front brake	180 × 30	180 × 30	200 × 20(2)	180 × 30 **14**
Rear brake	180 × 30	180 × 30	180 × 36	180 × 30
Front suspension	teles	teles	teles	teles
Rear suspension	s/a	s/a	s/a	s/a
Ignition system	coil **15**	coil **15**	magneto	coil
Wheelbase (in.)	51·0	51·0	51·0	52·4 **16**
Ground clear. (in.)	6·5 **17**	6·5 **17**	4·9	5·9 **18**
Width (in.)	31·9	31·9	22·8	32·3 **19**
Length (in.)	78·9	78·9	75·4	77·6 **20**
Dry weight (lb)	329	329	240	330 **21**

1 1974—7·5 **2** 1973—28/7500 **3** 1973—2·7 **4** late—112 **5** late—65 **6** 25 for CDI system **7** 3·29 for CDI **8** 1973—14/48 **9** 1973—7·31 **10** 1976—KH250-A, 1976/80—KH250-B **11** 1973 only—15 **12** late 1975—3·25 × 18 **13** late 1975—3·50 × 18 **14** 1976, B Model—226 disc **15** CDI for USA models from 1969 **16** 1974—54·1 **17** late—6·7 **18** 1976—6·1 **19** 1978—29·9 **20** 1974—79·7, 1976 B model—82·1 **21** 1974—339, 1976 A model—348, 1976 B model—353

Model	S2	S3 1	H1 2	H2
Year from	**1971**	**1973**	**1968**	**1971**
Year to	**1973**	**1980**	**1976**	**1975**
No. cylinders	3	3	3	3
Bore (mm)	53	57	60	71
Stroke (mm)	52·3	52·3	58·8	63
Capacity (cc)	346	400·4	498·8	748
Compression ratio (to 1)	7·3	6·5	6·8	7·0
Induction	piston	piston	piston	piston
bhp	45 **3**	42 **4**	60 **5**	74 **6**
@ rpm	8000	7000	7500 **5**	6800
torque (Kg-m)	4·25 **7**	4·32 **8**	5·85 **9**	7·9 **10**
@ rpm	7000 **7**	6500	7000 **9**	6500
Starting system	kick	kick	kick	kick
Oil system	pump	pump	pump	pump
Port timing:				
Inlet	73	73	76	75
Transfer	58	58	59·5	58
Exhaust	89	86	89	89
Ignition timing degree	23	23	25 **11**	23
Ignition timing (mm)	2·6	2·6	3·46 **11**	3·14

Model	S2	S3 1	H1 2	H2
Year from	**1971**	**1973**	**1968**	**1971**
Year to	**1973**	**1980**	**1976**	**1975**
Primary drive gearing	27/60	27/60	27/65	32/60
Final drive gearing	14/43	14/41 **12**	15/45 **13**	15/47
Box gearing: top	0·96	0·96	0·81	0·81
Box gearing: 4th	1·12	1·12	0·92	0·92
Box gearing: 3rd	1·35	1·35	1·09	1·11
Box gearing: 2nd	1·79	1·79	1·40	1·47
Box gearing: 1st	2·86	2·86	2·20	2·17
O/A top gear ratio	6·55	6·25 **14**	5·85 **15**	4·76
No. gears	5	5	5	5
Fuel (l)	14	14	15 **16**	17
Engine oil (l)	1·5	1·5	2·3	2·0
Box oil (l)	1·1	1·1	1·2	1·4
Front fork/leg (cc)	210	155 **17**	230 **18**	160 **19**
Front tyre	3·00 × 18	3·25 × 18	3·25 × 19	3·25 × 19
Rear tyre	3·50 × 18	3·50 × 18	4·00 × 18	4·00 × 18
Front brake	180 × 30 **20**	277 disc	200 × 35 **21**	296 disc
Rear brake	180 × 30	180 × 30	180 × 35	200 × 35
Front suspension	teles	teles	teles	teles
Rear suspension	s/a	s/a	s/a	s/a
Ignition system	coil	coil **22**	CDI **23**	CDI
Wheelbase (in.)	51·6 **24**	53·7	55·1 **25**	55·5 **26**
Ground clear. (in.)	6·3	5·9	5·3 **27**	6·9 **28**
Width (in.)	30·3 **29**	32·3 **30**	33·1 **31**	33·5 **32**
Length (in.)	78·7 **33**	79·7 **34**	82·5 **35**	81·9 **36**
Dry weight (lb)	335	353 **37**	383 **38**	423 **39**

1 1976—KH400-A **2** 1976—KH500-A8 **3** 1973—44 **4** 1976—38 **5** 1973—59/8000, 1976—52/7000 **6** 1973—71 **7** 1973—4·0/7500 **8** 1976—3·9 **9** 1973—5·7/7000, 1976—5·4/6500 **10** 1973—7·7, 1974—7·9 **11** 1972—20/2·23, 1973 early—25/3·46, 1973 late—23/2·94 (H1D on) **12** 1973 Europe—14/37, 1976—15/41 **13** Europe—16/45 **14** 1973 Europe—5·64, 1976—5·83 **15** Europe—5·48 **16** 1973—16 **17** 1976—212, 1978—185 **18** 1973 early (H1C)—160, 1974—170, 1976—175 **19** 1975—175 **20** 1973—277 disc **21** 1972—296 disc **22** 1976—CDI **23** 1972—coil, 1973 early—CDI **24** 1973, some—52·4 **25** 1973—55·5 **26** 1974—56·5, 1975—57·0 **27** 1973—5·7 **28** 1974—6·3, 1975—5·5 **29** 1973, some 32·3 **30** Europe—29·9 **31** 1973—32·9, Europe—32·5 **32** 1974—33·9, 1975—32·7 **33** 1973, some 77·6 **34** Europe—80·9, 1978—80·9, 1978 USA—79·7 **35** 1973—82·1, Europe—83·7 **36** 1974—83·1, 1975 Europe—85·6 **37** 1973 Italy—381, 1976—357, 1976 Europe—364 **38** 1973—408, 1976—423, Europe—428 **39** 1974—448, 1975—452, Europe—458

Model	H1R	H1R-A	H2R
Year from	**1969**	**1971**	**1973**
Year to	**1970**		**1974**
No. cylinders	3	3	3
Bore (mm)	60	60	71
Stroke (mm)	58·8	58·8	63
Capacity (cc)	499	499	748
Compression ratio (to 1)	7·5	8·0	6·7

Model	H1R	H1R-A	H2R
Year from	**1969**	**1971**	**1973**
Year to	**1970**		**1974**
Induction	piston	piston	piston
bhp	75	80	100 +
@ rpm	9000	9500	9000
torque (Kg-m)			8·3
@ rpm			8500
Starting system	push	push	push
Oil system	pump & mix	pump & mix	pump & mix
Port timing:			
Inlet	81	85	78
Transfer	63	70	63·5
Exhaust	97	101	96·5
Ignition timing degree	25	25	23
Ignition timing (mm)	3·45	3·45	3·0
Primary drive gearing	27/65	27/65	32/60
Final drive gearing	15/32 std	15/32 std	15/41
Box gearing: top	0·92	0·92	0·826
Box gearing: 4th	1·00	1·00	0·90
Box gearing: 3rd	1·136	1·136	1·048
Box gearing: 2nd	1·40	1·40	1·294
Box gearing: 1st	1·882	1·882	1·714
O/A top gear ratio	4·725	4·725	4·234
No. gears	5	5	5
Fuel (l)	22·7	22·7	24
Engine oil (l)	0·5	0·5	1·0
Box oil (l)	1·6	1·6	1·7
Front fork/leg (cc)	150	150	147
Front tyre	3·00 × 18	3·00 × 18	3·00 × 18
Rear tyre	3·50 × 18	3·50 × 18	3·30 × 18
Front brake	twin drum	twin drum	dual 296 disc
Rear brake	drum	drum	230 × 48
Front suspension	teles	teles	teles
Rear suspension	s/a	s/a	s/a
Ignition system	coil	CDI	CDI
Wheelbase (in.)			54·4
Ground clear. (in.)			5·9
Width (in.)			21·3
Length (in.)	75·4	75·4	78·9
Dry weight (lb)	300	293	315

Model	W1	W1S	W2	W3
Year from	**1965**	**1967**	**1967**	**1972**
Year to	**1968**	**1971**	**1970**	**1975**
No. cylinders	2	2	2	2
Bore (mm)	74	74	74	74
Stroke (mm)	72·6	72·6	72·6	72·6

Model	W1	W1S	W2	W3
Year from	**1965**	**1967**	**1967**	**1972**
Year to	**1968**	**1971**	**1970**	**1975**
Capacity (cc)	624	624	624	624
Compression ratio (to 1)	8·7	9·0	9·0	9·0
Valve type	ohv	ohv	ohv	ohv
bhp	50	53	53	53
@ rpm	6500	7000	7000	7000
torque (Kg-m)	5·7	5·7	5·7	5·7
@ rpm	5500	5500	5500	5500
Starting system	kick	kick	kick	kick
Oil system	dry sump	dry sump	dry sump	dry sump
Valve timing:				
Inlet opens BTDC	40	40	40	40
Inlet closes ABDC	60	60	60	60
Exhaust opens BBDC	80	80	80	80
Exhause closes ATDC	30	30	30	30
Tappets, inlet (mm)	0·06	0·06	0·06	0·06
Tappets, exhaust (mm)	0·06	0·06	0·06	0·06
Ignition timing degree	5–31	5–31	5–31	5–31
Primary drive gearing	23/52	23/52	23/52	23/52
Final drive gearing	19/41	18/42	18/42	18/42
Box gearing: top	1·00	1·00	1·00	1·00
Box gearing: 3rd	1·22	1·22	1·22	1·22
Box gearing: 2nd	1·71	1·71	1·71	1·71
Box gearing: 1st	2·54	2·54	2·54	2·54
O/A top gear ratio	4·88	5·27	5·27	5·27
No. gears	4	4	4	4
Fuel (l)	15	15	15	15
Engline oil (l)	2·5	2·5	2·5	2·5 **1**
Box oil (l)	0·5	0·5	0·5	0·5
Front fork/leg (cc)	280	280	280	165
Front tyre	3·25 × 18	3·25 × 19	3·25 × 19	3·25 × 19
Rear tyre	3·50 × 18	4·00 × 18	4·00 × 18	4·00 × 18
Front brake	200 × 35	200 × 35	200 × 35	dual 245 disc
Rear brake	180 × 35	180 × 35	180 × 35	180 × 35
Front suspension	teles	teles	teles	teles
Rear suspension	s/a	s/a	s/a	s/a
Ignition system	coil	coil	coil	coil
Wheelbase (in.)	55·7	55·9	55·7	55·9
Ground clear. (in)	5·5	5·7	5·9	5·5
Width (in.)	34·6	34·1	34·6	33·5 **2**
Length (in.)	83·7	84·4	83·3	84·1 **3**
Dry weight (lb)	398	437	398	467 **4**

1 1974—3·0 **2** 1974—33·9 **3** 1974—84·6 **4** 1974—425

Model	Z2	Z1	Z900	Z900 LTD
Year from	**1973**	**1972**	**1976**	**1976**
Year to	**1974**	**1975**		
No cylinders	4	4	4	4
Bore (mm)	64	66	66	66
Stroke (mm)	58	66	66	66
Capacity (cc)	746	903	903	903
Compression ratio (to 1)	9·0	8·5	8·5	8·5
Valve type	dohc	dohc	dohc	dohc
bhp	69	82	81	81
@ rpm	9000	8500	8500	8500
torque (Kg-m)	5·9	7·5	7·3	7·3
@ rpm	7500	7000	7500	7500
Starting system	elec, kick	elec, kick	elec, kick	elec, kick
Oil system	wet sump	wet sump	wet sump	wet sump
Valve timing:				
Inlet opens BTDC	30	30	30	30
Inlet closes ABDC	70	70	70	70
Exhaust opens BBDC	70	70	70	70
Exhaust closes ATDC	30	30	30	30
Tappets (mm)	0·05—0·1	0·05—0·1	0·05—0·1	0·05—0·1
Ignition timing degree	20–40	5–40 **1**	20–40	20–40
Primary drive gearing	56/97	56/97	56/97	56/97
Final drive gearing	15/42	15/35	15/35	15/35
Box gearing: top	1·22	1·22	1·22	1·22
Box gearing: 4th	1·38	1·38	1·38	1·38
Box gearing: 3rd	1·67	1·67	1·67	1·67
Box gearing: 2nd	2·19	2·19	2·19	2·19
Box gearing: 1st	3·17	3·17	3·17	3·17
O/A top gear ratio	5·92	4·93	4·93	4·93
No. gears	5	5	5	5
Fuel (1)	17	18 **2**	17	13
Engine oil (1)	3·7	3·7	3·7	3·7
Front fork/leg (cc)	170	170	174	
Front tyre	3·25 × 19	3·25 × 19	3·25 × 19	ML 90–19
Rear tyre	4·00 × 18	4·00 × 18	4·00 × 18	MT 90–16
Front brake	296 disc	296 disc	dual 245 disc	dual 245 disc
Rear brake	200 × 35	200 × 35	200 × 35	230 disc
Front suspension	teles	teles	teles	teles
Rear suspension	s/a	s/a	s/a	s/a
Ignition system	coil	coil	coil	coil
Wheelbase (in.)	59·1	58·7	58·7	59·5
Ground clear. (in.)	6·5	6·5	6·5	
Width (in.)	34·1	34·1	34·1	28
Length (in.)	86·6	86·8 **3**	86·8	
Dry weight (lb)	506	506 **4**	514	543 wet

1 late 1974—20 to 40 **2** 1975—16 **3** Europe—88·4 **4** 1975—511

Model	M10/M11	J1	J1T	J1TR
Year from	**1965**	**1965**	**1965**	**1965**
Year to	**1969**	**1968**	**1967**	**1967**
No. cylinders	1	1	1	1
Capacity (cc)	50/52	85	85	85
Power: bhp	4·5	7·5	7·8	8
@ rpm	7500	6800	7000	7000
Valve type	piston	disc	disc	disc
No. gears	3	4	4	4
Tyre (in.)	2·25 × 17	2·50 × 17	2·50 × 17	2·50 × 17
Brake type	drum	drum	drum	drum
Front suspension	teles	teles	teles	teles
Rear suspension	s/a	s/a	s/a	s/a

Model	G1	G1TRL	G1M	D1
Year from	**1966**	**1967**	**1967**	**1966**
Year to	**1969**	**1969**	**1968**	**1968**
No. cylinders	1	1	1	1
Capacity (cc)	90	90	90	100
Power: bhp	8·2	8·2	16	10
@ rpm	6500	6500	9000	7000
Valve type	disc	disc	disc	disc
No. gears	4	4	4	4
Front tyre (in.)	2·50 × 17	2·50 × 17	2·50 × 17	2·50 × 17
Rear tyre (in.)	2·50 × 17	2·50 × 17	2·75 × 17	2·50 × 17
Brake type	drum	drum	drum	drum
Front suspension	teles	teles	teles	teles
Rear suspension	s/a	s/a	s/a	s/a

Model	C1	C2SS	C2TR	B8
Year from	**1966**	**1967**	**1967**	**1962**
Year to	**1967**	**1968**	**1968**	**1966**
No. cylinders	1	1	1	1
Capacity (cc)	120	120	120	125
Power: bhp	10	11·5	11·5	8 to 11
@ rpm	7000	7000	7000	6000
Valve type	disc	disc	disc	piston
No. gears	4	4	4	4
Front tyre (in.)	2·50 × 17	2·50 × 18	2·75 × 18	3·00 × 16
Rear tyre (in.)	2·50 × 17	2·75 × 18	2·75 × 18	3·00 × 16
Brake type	drum	drum	drum	drum
Front suspension	teles	teles	teles	teles
Rear suspension	s/a	s/a	s/a	s/a

Model	**B8T**	**B8M**	**B8S**	**Meguro Ranger**
Year from	**1964**	**1963**	**1964**	**1962**
Year to	**1966**	**1964**	**1966**	
No. cylinders	1	1	1	1
Capacity (cc)	125	125	150	164
Power: bhp	11		12	
@ rpm	6000		6500	
Valve type	piston	piston	piston	ohv
No. gears	4	4	4	
Front tyre (in.)	trail		3·00 × 16	2·75 × 17
Rear tyre (in.)	trail		3·00 × 16	3·00 × 17
Brake type	drum	drum	drum	drum
Front suspension	teles	teles	teles	teles
Rear suspension	s/a	s/a	s/a	s/a

Model	**F1**	**F1TR**	**F2**	**F2TR**
Year from	**1965**	**1965**	**1966**	**1966**
Year to	**1966**	**1966**	**1969**	**1967**
No. cylinders	1	1	1	1
Capacity (cc)	175	175	175	175
Power: bhp	17	17	18	18
@ rpm	7000	7000	7000	7000
Valve type	piston	piston	disc	disc
No. gears	4	4 × 2	4	4
Front tyre (in.)	2·50 × 18	2·50 × 18	2·50 × 18	2·75 × 18
Rear tyre (in.)	2·75 × 18	2·75 × 18	2·75 × 18	3·00 × 18
Brake type	drum	drum	drum	drum
Front suspension	teles	teles	teles	teles
Rear suspension	s/a	s/a	s/a	s/a

Model	**F3**	**F4**	**F21M**	**F11M**
Year from	**1968**	**1968**	**1966**	**1972**
Year to	**1970**	**1970**	**1970**	**1973**
No. cylinders	1	1	1	1
Capacity (cc)	175	250	250	247
Power: bhp	20	23	30	29·5
@ rpm	7300	7500	7000	7500
Valve type	disc	disc	disc	piston
No. gears	4	4	4	5
Front tyre (in.)	3·00 × 19	3·25 × 19	3·25 × 19	3·00 × 21
Rear tyre (in.)	3·50 × 18	4·00 × 18	4·00 × 18	4·00 × 18
Brake type	drum	drum	drum	drum
Front suspension	teles	teles	teles	teles
Rear suspension	s/a	s/a	s/a	s/a

Colours, model recognition, engine and frame numbers

In many cases Kawasaki models had black frames and detail painted parts with just the petrol tank coloured. Where fitted the side covers would be in the same finish while the mudguards could be painted to match the tank, chrome plated or in stainless steel. The tank and side cover marking was usually changed each year to give a new style.

The model noted are a precis of the main text and engine and frame numbers are included for reference (En = engine, Fr = frame). The notes are arranged by capacity, model and year.

M10, M11
1965–69
Rocket red or black for whole machine, chrome tank panels. Spine frame, inclined engine, **M10** is 50 cc, **M11** is 52 cc.
En: 700 001, Fr: M10-00 001

MT1
1970–71
Lime green tank and front guard, rest black. Compact fold-up model, external fork springs, very short front guard.
En: MTE 00 001, Fr: MT-00 001
1972
MT1A Bright orange. Internal fork springs.
En and Fr as 1970.
1973
MT1A Orange.
En and Fr as 1970.
1974
MT1B Candy lime. Longer front guard
En: MTE 29090, Fr: MT-29588
1975
MT1C Vivid yellow. Front brake backplate moved to right side.
En: MTE 37203, Fr: MT-38475

J1, J1D, J1L
1964–68
Tank and front guard in black, maroon, Balboa blue or rocket red. Disc valve single, spine frame, **J1D** with electric start, **J1L** with pump oiling.
J1—En: J1E 00001, Fr: 100 001
J1L—En: LFE 00001, Fr: J1L-00001

J1T, J1TL
1965–67
Colour as **J1**. Touring version with upswept exhaust, white-wall tyres, sports front guard, open chainguard, **J1TL** with pump oiling.
En: (J1T) 00001, Fr: J1T 00001
En: (J1TL) 00001, Fr: J1TL 00001

J1TR, J1TRL
1965–67
Red tank and frame, chrome front guard. Trail version of **J1T**, universal tyres, skid plate, sprung front guard, **J1TRL** with pump oiling.
En: 00001, Fr: J1RL 00001

J1M
1965–67
Moto-cross version of J1 series.

G1, G1L, G1DL, G1TRL
1966–69
Tank in black, maroon, Balboa blue or rocket red, stainless front guard. 90 cc version of J series, **G1L** with pump oiling, **G1DL** with this and electric start, **G1TRL** trial version.
G1—En: 100 001, Fr: 100 0001
G1L—En: 300 001, Fr: 110 0001

G1M
1967–68
Red tank, stainless front guard, black frame. Motocross version of G1, upswept expansion box.
En: 400 001, Fr: G1-400 001

GA1
1968–70
Black tank, stainless front guard, frame. Duplex cradle frame, fork gaiters.
En: GAE-000 001, Fr: GA-200 001
1971–74
GA1A Tank pearl candy red or blue with white lower section and side covers, stainless guards. No fork gaiters, new seat.
En: GAE-000 000, Fr: GA-200 000

GA2
1968–70
Tank and side covers candy red or blue, black frame, stainless guards. 5 speed version of **GA1**, chainguard only.
En: GAE-200 001, Fr: GA-200 001
1971–74
GA2A Colour as **GA1A**, same changes, numbers as **GA2.**

GA3
1968-1970
Pastel orange tank, white side cover, stainless guards, black frame. Street scrambler version of **GA2** with universal front tyre and upswept exhaust. Numbers as **GA2.**

MC1
1973
Candy red tank, red guards, black frame. Trail bike with lights, skid plate, trail tyres, sprung front guard.
En: MCE000 001, Fr: MC-000 001
1974
MC1A Candy ocean blue tank, blue guards. New seat, left engine cover extended, brake wear indicators.
En: MCE 006966, Fr: MC-006946
1975
MC1B Blue or red as earlier years. Rear tyre section changed to 3·00 in.
En: MCE 018500, Fr: MC-018500

MC1M
1973–74
Tank candy lime, guards and frame black. Moto-cross version of **MC1**, competition tyres.
En: MCE 500001, Fr: MC-500001
1975
MC1MA Colour as 1973.
En: MCE 509500, Fr: MC-509500

G2S
1973–74
Tank and side covers metallic black, candy super red or candy ocean blue, stainless front guard. Similar to **GA1**, drum air cleaner housing, full chaincase.
En: G8E-000000, Fr: G8-000001

G2T
1973–76
Colour as **G2S**. Based on **GA2**, otherwise as **G2S**.
En: G8E 500000, Fr: G8-500001

G3TR
1968–70
Pastel orange tank, stainless guards. Trial version of **GA2**, upswept exhaust.
En: G3E 00001, Fr: GA-200001

G3SS
1968–70
Tank pastel and candy blue, stainless guards. Similar to **GA2**.
En: GAE 000000, Fr: GA-000000
1971
G3SSA Tank and side covers light yellow or bright orange. New fuel tank and side covers.
En: GAE 268738, Fr: GA-268327
1972
G3SSB Tank and side covers pearl candy red. New fuel tank.
En: GAE 280935, Fr: GA-306826
1973
G3SSC Tank and side covers candy orange. Change to air cleaner and seat, revised plug grade.
En: GAE 292961, Fr: GA-329103
1974
G3SSD Tank and side covers candy lime. Changes to fuel tank, side covers, rear guard and front tyre section, brake wear indicators added.
En: GAE 507550, Fr: GA-355001
1975
G3SSE Tank and side covers candy halibut red. Capacity increased to 100 cc, kill and front brake switches added, tyre sections increased late in year.
En: G7E 518987, Fr: GA-361514

D1
1966–68
Tank black, maroon, Balboa blue or rocket red, chrome

front guard. 100 cc version of **G1**, white lines on tyres, upswept exhaust.
En: 300001, Fr: D1-2100001

G31M
1969–71
Lime green tank, light alloy guards. Motocross version of **G3TR**, expansion box.
En: G31E 00001, Fr: G31-00001

G3TRA
1971
Tank and side covers bright orange, stainless guards. 100 cc version of **G3TR** with different tank, side covers, exhaust and front guard.
En: G3E 000001, Fr: GA-272967

G4TR
1969–70
Tank candy red, stainless guards. Trail bike with high level exhaust, dual range gearbox, duplex frame, skid plate.
En: G4E 000001, Fr: G4-000001
1971
G4TRA Tank pearl candy red. Chrome heat shield on silencer.
En: G4E 014462, Fr: G4-014460
1972
G4TRB Tank pearl candy orange, chrome guards. Dual range shift lever moved to right bar.
En: G4E 029960, Fr: G4-036049
1973
G4TRC Tank candy red, chrome guards, black cylinder and head. Turn signals and steering lock fitted as standard.
En: G4E 046102, Fr: G4-052153
1974
G4TRD Tank candy super red. New tank and rear chainguard, 100 emblem on silencer heat shield.
En: G4E 064001, Fr: G4-070001
1975
G4TRE Tank and guards vivid yellow.
En: G4E 077300, Fr: G4-083000

G4TRA
1974
Tank and guards candy orange. Modified **G4TR** with protection bars and equipped with spade.
En: G4E 064001, Fr: G4-070001
1975
G4TRAA Tank and guards vivid yellow.
En: G4E 077300, Fr: G4-083000

G5
1971–72
Tank, front guard and seat tail yellow. Trail model with upswept exhaust.
En: G5E 000001, Fr: G5-000001
1973
G5A Colour orange or candy blue. Turn signals fitted as standard, larger diameter front tyre.
En: G5E 022055, Fr: G5-022027
1974
G5B Colour candy orange or candy blue. Brake wear indicator added.
En: G5E 045001, Fr: G5-045001
1975
G5C Colour candy red or candy gold. Choke lever moved from left bar.
En: G5E 069700, Fr: G5-070500

GA5A
1971–74
Tank and side panels candy gold, candy blue or melamine candy red, chrome guards. Developed from **GA2**, duplex cradle frame.
En: G3E-00001, Fr: GA-200000

G7T
1972–74
Tank and side panels metallic black, candy super red, candy gold or candy ocean blue, chrome guards. Light road model, duplex cradle frame, cylindrical air cleaner.
En: G7E 500001, Fr: G7-500001
1975–76
G7TA Colours as 1972. Charge rate switch deleted.
En: G7E 532456, Fr: G7-518658
G7S
1973–74
Colours as 1972 **G7T**. 4 speed version of **G7T**.
En: G7E 000001, Fr: G7-000001
1975
G7SA Colours as 1973. Charge rate switch deleted.
En: G7E 000000, Fr: G7-000000

G3T
1974–76
Tank candy halibut red or candy blue, stainless guards. Much as **G7T** but drum air cleaner.
En: G7E 520001, Fr: GF3-00001

C1, C1L, C1D, C1DL
1966–67
Black finish, stainless front guard. Pressed steel spine frame, **L** models have oil pump, **D** models have electric starter.
En: 300001, Fr: C1-1100001

C2TR
1967–68
Tank candy red or candy blue with light colour tank panels and side covers, chrome guards. Trial version of **C** model with quick change gearing, skid plate, trail tyres, raised exhaust.
En: 300001, Fr: C2-6100001

C2SS
1967–68
Colour as **C2TR**. Street scrambler version of **C2TR** with unsprung front guard, road tyres, no carrier and no quick change gearing.
En: 300001, Fr: C2-3100001

B8, B8T
1962–66
Tank and front guard black or metallic black, rest black, chrome tank panels, light finish to chaincase. Pressed steel frame, single seat, carrier, **B8T** was touring version.
En: FE 00001, Fr: B8-00001

B1, B1L, B1LA
1965–76
Tank maroon, melamine candy blue, black, melamine candy red or rocket red, chrome tank panels, stainless front guard for later models but early ones painted to match tank. Spine frame, road 125, **L** models with oil pump.
En: B1L 300001, Fr: B1-1100001

B1T, B1TL
1965–69
Tank black, maroon or rocket red with chrome panels, stainless front guard. Touring version of **B1** with upswept exhaust, different seat, gaitered forks, **L** model with oil pump.
En: 300001, Fr: B1-2100001

F6
1970–71
Tank and guards deep yellow. Trail model with upswept exhaust, universal tyres and sprung front guard.
En: F6E 00001, Fr: F6F-00001
1972
F6A Tank and guards orange.
En: F6E 12341, Fr: F6F-18361
1973
F6B Tank and guards red. New tank and seat, turn signals fitted as standard.
En: F6E 24447, Fr: F6F-30402

MB1
1969–71
Pearl ivory tank, chrome guards. Pull start, side valve engine in duplex, rigid frame, single speed, scooter disc wheels.

B8S
1964–66
Tank and front guard black, maroon, Balboa blue or red, light finish to chaincase. 150 cc version of **B8**.
En: BE8S 00001, Fr: 8F8-00001

F1
1965–66
Tank black or rocket red with chrome panels, stainless front guard. 175 cc version of **B8** with electric starter.
En: 100001, Fr: F1-10001

F1TR
1965–66
Tank black or rocket red with chrome panels, chrome front guard. Trail version of **F1** with dual gear range, competition tyres and skidplate. Retained electric starter.
En: 200001, Fr: F1-20001

F2
1966–69
Chrome front guard, rest black, rocket red or melamine candy red. Similar to **F1** but with disc valve engine.
En: 300001, Fr: F21-00001

F2TR
1966–67
Colour as **F2**. Trail version of **F2** similar to **F1TR**.
En: 500001, Fr: F22-00001

F3
1968–70
Tank and side covers alumitone silver, chrome guards. Trail format with disc valve engine, raised exhaust but unsprung front guard, dual sprockets.
En: F3E 00001, Fr: F3-100001

F7

1970–71

Deep yellow tank and guards. Trial bike with rear carrier, sprung front guard with mud-flap, Hatta front fork.
En: F7E 00001, Fr: F7F-00001

1972

F7A Tank and guards red. 175 emblem on oil tank.
En: F7E 19268, Fr: F7-25706

1973

F7B Tank and guards bright orange or candy blue. Change to tank and seat, turn signals fitted as standard.
En: F7E 44158, Fr: F7-50556

1974

F7C Tank and guards metallic silver or candy blue. Change to tank, seat and tail-light, tail piece added to silencer.
En: F7E 67001, Fr: F7-73001

1975

F7D Tank candy green or candy brown, guards metallic silver.
En: F7E 90600, Fr: F7-96287

SG

1964–69

Black, chrome tank decoration. Early road single, cantilever saddle, rear carrier, electric starter.
En: SGE-0001, Fr: SG-0001

F21M

1966–70

Tank lime green or candy red, chrome guards. Moto-cross model, disc valve engine, expansion chamber.
En: 400001, Fr: F24-0001

F4

1968–70

Tank midnight blue or pastel orange, guards chrome or stainless. Trail machine but unsprung front guard, qd lights, raised exhaust.
En: F4E 00001, Fr: F4-00001

F8

1970–71

Tank and guards bright orange or tank ivory and guards lime green. Trial machine based on **F4** with Hatta forks and alloy sprocket.
En: F8E 00001, Fr: F8-00001

1972

F8A Colours as 1970.
En: F8E 09786, Fr: F8-09554

F81M

1970–71

Tank and guards lime green. Moto-cross version of **F8**.
En: F81E-00001, Fr: F81-00001

F11

1971–72

Tank, front guard and seat tail yellow or candy red. Trail successor to **F8**, alloy rims.
En: F11E 00001, Fr: F11-00001

1973

F11 Colours as 1971. Change to seat, tail piece added to silencer.
En: F11E 00555, Fr: F11-00540

1974

F11A Colours candy lime or candy yellow. New engine covers, brake wear indicator added.
En: F11E 16501, Fr: F11-16501

1975

F11B Tank candy ocean blue, candy blue or candy orange, front guard and seat tail metallic silver.
En: F11E 31700, Fr: F11-31686

F11M

1972–73

Tank lime green, guards black. Moto-cross version of **F11** with duplex frame in special steel, plastic tank, limited production.
En: F11E 90001, Fr: F11-90001

A1

1966–68

Tank upper, headlight shell, fork lamp brackets and rear unit top covers in candy red or candy blue, lower tank in white, side covers in silver, guards painted to match tank or front stainless and rear chrome, black frame. Twin cylinder, disc valves, instruments in headlamp shell.
En: A1E 00001, Fr: A1-00001

1969

A1 Colours as 1966 in new style with panelled tank, guards stainless and chrome. Change to tank, seat, rear units, CDI for USA models, separate instrument mounting.
En: A1E 00000, Fr: A1-00000

1970

A1A Tank pearl candy red, stainless guards. Change to tank, seat and rear guard.
En: A1E 15311, Fr: A1-13519

1971
A1B Tank pearl ivory, stainless guards.
En: A1E 21044, Fr: A1-17477

A1SS
1967–68
Tank upper, headlight shell and fork lamp brackets in candy red or candy blue, lower tank in white, side cover silver, front guard stainless, rear guard chrome, frame black. Street scrambler version of **A1** with both exhausts upswept on left, braced bars, instruments in headlamp shell.
En: A1E 00001, Fr: A1-00001
1969
A1SS Tank and side cover candy red or candy blue, guards as 1967. CDI adopted, separate instruments.
En: A1E 00000, Fr: A1-00000
1970
A1SSA Tank and side cover pastel yellow or pastel white, guards stainless. Change to tank, seat and rear guard.
En: A1E 15561, Fr: A1-68053
1971
A1SSB Tank and side cover pearl ivory, guards stainless, matt black exhaust system.
En: A1E 21067, Fr: A1-69822
A1R
Red tank, stainless front guard. Road racing version of **A1**.
En: A1E 50001, Fr: A1-50001

S1
1971–72
Tank, front guard, side covers, tail piece in pearl white or pearl candy red. Triple, separate bar holder, friction steering damper, drum front brake.
En: S1E 00001, Fr: S1F-00001
1973
S1A Tank, side covers and tail in candy orange, candy blue or candy gold, chrome guards. Change to seat and front guard.
En: S1E 05494, Fr: S1F-04691
1974
S1B Colour candy green. Change to seat, brake wear indicator added, friction steering damper dropped.
En: S1E 12001, Fr: S1F-12001
1975
S1C Colour halibut blue.
En: S1E 17100, Fr: S1F-16300

1976
KH250-A5 Colour candy super red. New grips, locking tank cap, 3 fuse system.
En: S1E 026600, Fr: S1F-24400
1976
KH250-B1 Colour candy super red or candy sky blue. Disc front brake, frame parts as 400 model.
En: S1E 028801, Fr: KH250B-000001
1977
KH250-B2 Colours candy wine red or candy orient blue.
En: S1E 038401, Fr: KH250B-008601
1978
KH250-B3 Colours candy lime green or candy cobalt blue. New brake master cylinder and change to seat.
En: S1E 048301, Fr: KH250B-018501
1979
KH250-B4 Colours candy lime green, classic white or candy persimmon red.
En: S1E 054801, Fr: KH250B-025001
1980
KH250-B5 Colour lime green, KH on seat side.
En: S1E 058301, Fr: KH250B-028701

F5
1969–70
Tank and guards rawhide. Trial model, Hatta forks, CDI, alloy rims, diaphragm fuel tap.
En: F5E-00001, Fr: F5F-00001
1971
F5A Tank and guards lime green.
En: F5E-00000, Fr: F5F-00000

F9
1971-72
Tank and guards lime green. Developed from **F5**.
En: F5E-13666, Fr: F5F-13634
1973
F9A Colour as 1971. Turn signals fitted as standard.
En: F5E-24485, Fr: F9F-00001
1974
F9B Tank and guards candy gold. **F11** type front fork, brake wear indicator and silencer tail piece added.
En: F5E-32001, Fr: F9F-09001
1975
F9C Tank and guards metallic silver.
En: F5E-38600, Fr: F9F-15500

A7
1967–68
As 1966 **A1** except side covers match tank upper and guards not painted. larger version of **A1**.
En: A7E 00001, Fr: A7-00001
1969
A7 Colour and changes as 1969 **A1**.
En: A7E 00000, Fr: A7-00000
1970
A7A Colour and changes as 1970 **A1**.
En: A7E 17453, Fr: A7-18653
1971
A7B Colour as 1971 **A1.**
En: A7E 23043, Fr: A7-24200

A7SS
1967-68
Colour and details as 1967 **A1SS** except side cover painted to match tank upper.
En: A7E 00001, Fr: A7-00001
1969
A7SS Colour and changes as 1969 **A1SS**.
En: A7E 00000, Fr: A7-00000
1970
A7SSA Colour and changes as 1970 **A1SS**.
En: A7E 17557, Fr: A7-18753
1971
A7SSB Colour as 1971 **A1SS**.
En: A7E 22895, Fr: A7-24165

S2
1971–72
Colour and detail as 1971 S1 except larger capacity.
En: S2E 00001, Fr: S2F-00001
1973
S2A Colour as 1973 **S1A**. Change to seat and front fork, front disc brake.
En: S2E 28226, Fr: S2T-00001

S3
1973–74
Tank, side covers and tail candy red or candy sky blue, chrome guards. Enlarged version of **S2**, rubber engine mountings, different head fin shape.
En: S3E 00001, Fr: S3F-00001
1975
S3A Colours candy super red or candy green.
En: S3E 14300, Fr: S3F-14300
1976
KH400-A3 Colours dark green or orange. New grips, locking tank cap, water resistant brake pads, 3 fuse system, CDI.
En: S3E 026300, Fr: S3F-26200
1977
KH400-A4 Colours candy emerald green or candy royal purple.
En: S3E 033601, Fr: S3F-033601
1978
KH400-A5 Colours candy persimmon red or candy lime green. New seat and brake master cylinder.
En: S3E 042801, Fr: S3F-042801
1979
KH400-A6
Fr: S3F-045901
1980
KH400-A7 Final version

F12MX
1973
Tank lime green, guards black. Motocross model with CDI, low level exhaust.
En: 90001, Fr: 90001

H1
1968–69
Tank and side covers midnight white or peacock grey, stainless guards. Original triple with CDI except in Europe, two leading shoe front brake, air scoop for rear brake.
En: KAE-00001, Fr: KAF-00001
1970
H1 Colour candy red.
En: KAE-06315, Fr: KAF-06727
1971
H1A Colour candy blue. New fuel tank.
En: KAE-21876, Fr: KAF-23626
1972
H1B Tank, side covers and guards pearl candy orange.
Coil ignition, front disc brake, straight line steering damper.
En: KAE-54101, Fr: KAF-48763
1973
H1D Tank, side covers and tail candy lime, chrome guards. Change to tank and seat, **H2** type CDI adopted, friction steering damper and air scoop dropped.
En: KAE 00000, Fr: H1F-00001
1974
H1E Colour candy lime or candy red. New CDI type adopted crankcase check valves added.
En: KAE 87001, Fr: H1F-17001

1975
H1F Colour candy sky blue or candy green.
En: KAE 102400, Fr: H1F-32400
1976
KH500-A8 Colour deep burgundy or copper. Change to gear shift pattern, grips, water resistant brake pads, locking tank cap and 3 fuse system adopted.
En: KAE 117100, Fr: H1F-47000

H1R
1969–71
Tank, front guard and seat tail lime green. Limited production, road racing version of H1.
En: KAE-90001, Fr: KAF-90001

W1
1965–68
Tank, side covers and headlight shell black, candy blue or candy red, stainless guards. 650 cc twin with separate gearbox much as BSA A10, gear pedal on right, instruments in headlight shell.
En: W1E-00001, Fr: W1F-00001

W1SS
1968–71
Tank, side covers and headlight shell candy red, candy blue or pastel blue, stainless guards. Twin carburettors, tuck-and-roll seat, short tubular silencers, instruments in headlight shell.
En: W1E-00001, Fr: W1F-00001

W2SS
1967-70
Tank black, candy red or candy blue, stainless guards. Developed **W1**, separate instruments.
En: W1E-00001, Fr: W1F-00001

W2TT
1968–69
Tank candy red, candy blue or pastel blue, stainless guards. Silencer mounted high on left.
En: W1E-00001, Fr: W1F-00001

H2
1971–72
Tank, side covers, tail and front guard pearl candy blue, chrome rear guard. Largest triple, front disc brake, chain oiler, friction steering damper.
En: H2E 00001, Fr: H2F-00001
1973
H2A Colours candy gold or candy purple except chrome front guard.
En: H2E 23158, Fr: H2F-23671
1974
H2B Colours candy gold or candy lime. Straight line steering damper and crankcase check valves added.
En: H2E 32401, Fr: H2F-32201
1975
H2C Colours candy super red or candy purple. Straight line damper moved to left side.
En: H2E 42827, Fr: H2F-42547

Z1
1972–73
Tank, side covers and seat-tail candy yellow or candy brown with red tank panels, chrome guards, black finish to head and barrel. Twin overhead camshaft four, disc front brake, chain oil pump.
En: Z1E 020001, Fr: ZiF-20001
1974
Z1A Colour candy orange or candy yellow, natural engine finish. Stop light warning bulb, ignition and carburettor changes.
En: Z1E 020001, Fr: Z1F-020001
1975
Z1B Colour candy super blue or candy super red. Chain oil pump deleted, O ring rear chain, 2 piece head gasket.
En: Z1E 047500, Fr: Z1F-047500
1976
Z900-A4 Colour diamond dark green or diamond brown. 26 mm carburettors, twin front discs, locking fuel tank cap, stronger frame, raised gearing, 3 fuse system, audible turn signals, 4 way hazard flasher, revised warning lights.
En: Z1E 086001, Fr: Z1F-085701
1976
Z900-B1 or **Z900LTD** Classic red tank, side covers and tail, chrome guards, chainguard, instrument pod. Custom build with cast alloy wheels, 16 in. rear, fat tyres, twin front discs with calipers behind fork legs, single rear disc, 2 level seat, small tank, laid back bars, shortened front guard, 4 into 2 exhaust, no centre stand.
En: Z1E 108503, Fr: KZ900B-500011

Carburettor settings

Model	Year	Type	Main jet	Needle jet	Jet needle	Pilot jet	Cut-away	Air screw	Fuel level	Ident. mark
M50	1967–	15	70	E-4	3G1-3	15	2·5	1½		
MT1	1970–75	15	70	E-0	3G9-3	15	2·0	1½	5	
GA0	1969–									
GA1	1968–74									
GA2	1968–74									
GA3	1968–70	19	160	E-4	5I2-3	17·5	2·0	1½	4	
GA5	1970–74									
G3TR	1968–70									
G3SS	1968–72									
G3SS	1973–75	19	77·5	O-2/2	4EJ7-3	17·5	2·0	1¼	4	
GA4	1969–70	19	180	E-6	5J4-3	15	2·0	1¾	4	
MC1	1973–75	19	75	O-2/2	4EJ7-3	17·5	2·0	1½	4	
MC1M	1973–75									
G2S	1973–74	19	77·5	O-2/2	4EJ7-3	17·5	2·0	1¼	4	
G2T	1973–76									
G6	1972–74	19	77·5	O-2	4EJ7-3	17·5	2·0	1½	4	
G8S	1972–73	19	80	O-2/2	4EJ7-2	17·5	2·0	1¼	4	
G8T	1972–73									
G3TRA	1971	19	170	O-2	4L6-3	17·5	2·5	1¾	4	
G4TR	1969–72	19	180	E-6	5I1-3	17·5	2·5	1¾	4	
G4TR	1973	19	107·5	E-6	5I1-3	17·5	2·5	1¼	4	
G4TR	1974–75	19	75	O-4/2	4EJ7-2	17·5	2·0	1½	4	
G5	1971–73	19	102·5	E-4	5I1-4	17·5	2·5	1½	4	
G5	1974–75	19	75	O-2/2	4EJ7-3	17·5	2·0	1½	4	
G7S	1973–75	19	80	O-2	4EJ7-2	20	2·0	1¾	4	
G7T	1972–76									
G3T	1974–76	19	77·5	O-2	4EJ7-3	17·5	2·0	1½	4	
G31M	1969–71	24	180	O-6	4DG6-3	35	3·0	1½		
B1L	1965–76	22	190	O-0	4L6-2	30	2·0	1½		
F6	1970–73	24	125	O-2	4J13-3	25	2·5	1¾	5	
MB1	1969–71	BV181	72·5			45		1¼		
F7	1970–73	26	105	O-2	4EJ3-3	30	2·5	1½	5	
F7	1974–75	26	105	O-6	4EJ3-3	30	3·0	1¼	5	
SG	1964–69	24	240	O-8	5J1-3	20	2·0	1¾		

Model	Year	Type	Main jet	Needle jet	Jet needle	Pilot jet	Cut-away	Air screw	Fuel level	Ident. mark
F8	1970–72	30	117·5	O-8	5EL9-2	30	2·5	$1\frac{3}{4}$		
F11	1971	30	110	O-8	5DJ19-3	40	2·5	$1\frac{1}{2}$		
F11	1972–73	30	112·5	O-8	5DJ19-3	40	2·5	$1\frac{3}{4}$	3	
F11	1974–75	30	115	O-6/8	5DJ19-3	30	2·5	$1\frac{1}{2}$	3	
F81M	1970–71	30	130	O-6	5EH7-3	40	2·5	$1\frac{1}{4}$		
F5	1969–70	32	132·5	O-8	5FL11-2	35	2·5	$1\frac{1}{4}$		
F5	1971	32	132·5	O-8/2	5EJ11-3	12·5	1·0	$1\frac{1}{4}$		
F9	1971–72	32	120	O-6	5EJ13-3	10	1·5	2		
F9	1973	32	120	O-6	5EJ13-3	17·5	2·0	$1\frac{1}{2}$	5·5	
F9	1974–75	30	120	O-6	5EJ13-3	17·5	2·0	$1\frac{1}{2}$	5·5	
F12MX	1973	34	130	P-0	6DH3-3	40	2·5	1	6	
A1	1966–71	22	140	O-6	4J13-3	30	2·5	$1\frac{1}{2}$		
A1SS	1967–71									
A1R	1967–68	26	310	N-6	7F3-2		4·0	1		
A7	1967–71	28	97·5	O-4	5EI4-4	30	2·5	$1\frac{1}{2}$		
A7SS	1967–71									
A7R	1968	29								
S1	1971–72	22	75	O-0	4EJ8-3	20	2·0	$1\frac{3}{4}$	4	
S1A	1973	22	75	O-2	4EJ9-3	17·5	2·5	$1\frac{1}{4}$	4	
S1B	1974									
S1C	1975	22	75	O-2	4EJ9-3	20	2·5	$1\frac{1}{2}$	4	
KH250-A5	1976									
KH250-B	1976–80	22	75 or 67·5	O-2	4EJ9-3	20	2·5	$1\frac{1}{2}$	4	
S2	1971–73	24	85	O-2	4EJ4-3	25	2·0	$1\frac{1}{2}$	4	
S3	1973–75	26	85	O-2	4EJ4-3	22·5	2·0	$1\frac{3}{4}$	4	
KH400	1976	26	77·5	O-6	4EJ4-3	20	2·5	$1\frac{1}{4}$	5	
H1	1968–71	28	100	O-2	5GL-3	30	3·0	$1\frac{1}{4}$	3	KA1
H1	1968–71	28	90	O-2	5EH7-3	30	2·5	$1\frac{1}{2}$	3	KAE-1
H1B	1972	28	100	O-4/8	5DJ19-4	30	2·0	$1\frac{1}{2}$	3	KA4
H1B	1972	28	95	O-4	5DJ19-3	30	2·0	$1\frac{1}{2}$	3	KA5
H1C	1973	28	100	O-2	5GL3-3	30	3·0	$1\frac{1}{4}$	3	
H1D	1973	28	92·5	O-4/8	5DJ19-4	30	2·5	$1\frac{1}{4}$	3	KA6
H1E	1974									
H1F	1975									
KH500	1976	28	75	O-4	5DJ19-3	25	2·0	$1\frac{1}{2}$	3	KH5
H2	1971	30	105	O-6	5FL14-2	35	2·5	$1\frac{1}{4}$		H2-1
H2	1972	30	97·5	O-6/8	5EJ15-3	35	2·5	$1\frac{1}{2}$	3	H2-2
H2A	1973	30	97·5	O-6/8	5EJ15-3	35	2·5	$1\frac{1}{2}$	3	H2-4
H2B	1974	30	102·5	O-6/8	5EJ15-4	40	2·5	$1\frac{3}{4}$	3	H2-5
H2C	1975									
H1R	1969–70	35	L 320 C 310 R 330	Q-5	6H1-3	60	3·0	$\frac{1}{2}$		
H1RA	1971	35	350	Q-0	6F5-3	60	3·5	$\frac{1}{2}$		
H2R	1973–74	35	280	Q-0	9FR3-3	60	5·0	$\frac{1}{2}$		
W1	1965–68	31	440	P-0	5L1-4	50	2·5	1		

Model	Year	Type	Main jet	Needle jet	Jet needle	Pilot jet	Cut-away	Air screw	Fuel level	Ident. mark
W1S W2	1967–71 1967–70	28	220	O-4	5L1-3	30	2·0	$\frac{3}{4}$		
W3	1972–75	28	220	O-5	5L1-3	30	2·0	$\frac{3}{4}$	8	
Z2	1973	26	102·5	P-3	5J9-3	35	2·5	$1\frac{1}{4}$	3·5	
Z2A	1974	26	105	O-6	5J9-3	17·5	1·5	$1\frac{1}{4}$	3·5	
Z1	1972–73	28	112·5	P-8	5J9-3	20	2·5	$1\frac{1}{2}$	3·5	
Z1A Z1B	1974 1975	28	112·5	O-8	5J9-2	17·5	1·5	$1\frac{1}{4}$	3·5	
Z900 Z900 LTD	1976 1976	26	115	O-6	5DL31-3	17·5	1·5	$1\frac{1}{4}$	3	

Model charts

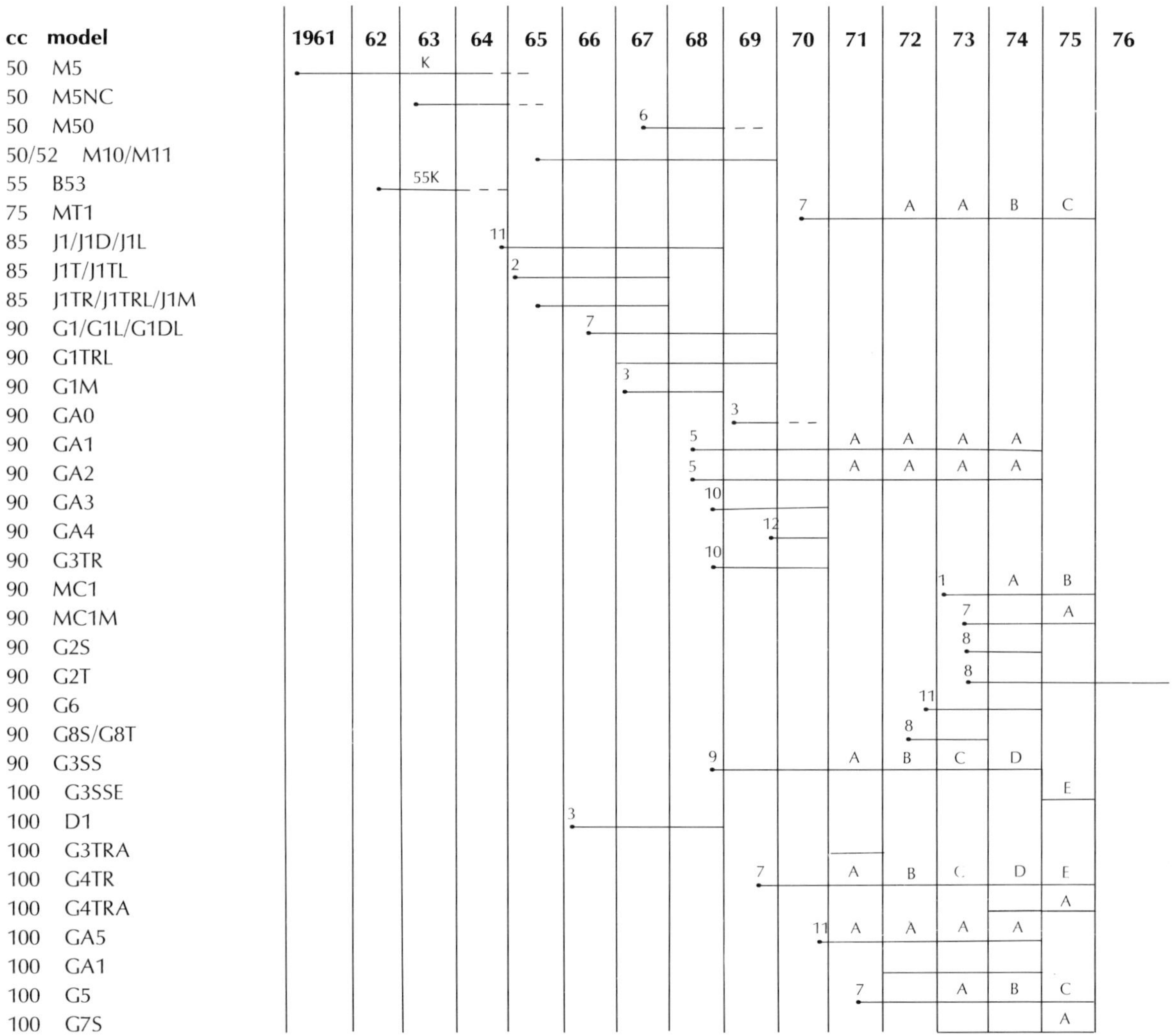

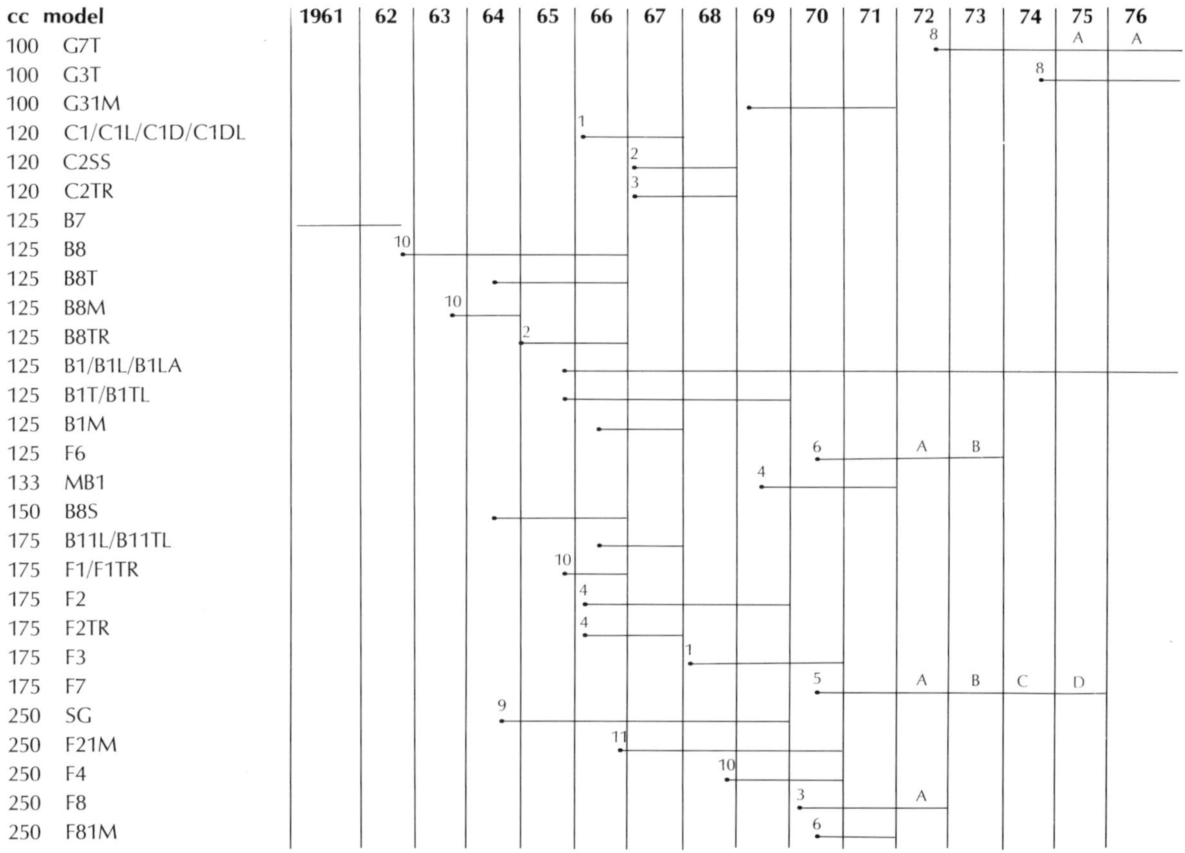
cc model
100 G7T
100 G3T
100 G31M
120 C1/C1L/C1D/C1DL
120 C2SS
120 C2TR
125 B7
125 B8
125 B8T
125 B8M
125 B8TR
125 B1/B1L/B1LA
125 B1T/B1TL
125 B1M
125 F6
133 MB1
150 B8S
175 B11L/B11TL
175 F1/F1TR
175 F2
175 F2TR
175 F3
175 F7
250 SG
250 F21M
250 F4
250 F8
250 F81M
1961 62 63 64 65 66 67 68 69 70 71 72 73 74 75 76

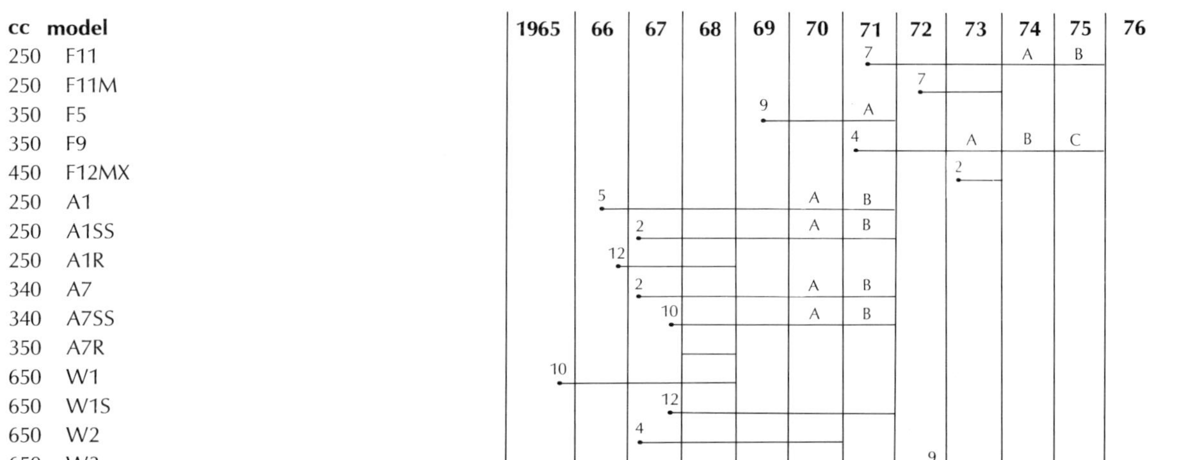
cc model
250 F11
250 F11M
350 F5
350 F9
450 F12MX
250 A1
250 A1SS
250 A1R
340 A7
340 A7SS
350 A7R
650 W1
650 W1S
650 W2
650 W3
1965 66 67 68 69 70 71 72 73 74 75 76

cc	model	1968	69	70	71	72	73	74	75	76	77	78	79	80
250	S1				3		A	B	C					
250	KH250-A									A5				
250	KH250-B									B1	B2	B3	B4	B5
350	S2				1		A							
400	S3						7		A					
400	KH400-A									A3	A4	A5	A6	A7
500	H1	9			A	B	D	E	F					
500	KH500-A									A8				
500	H1R		12											
750	H2				1		A	B	C					
750	H2R						3							
750	Z2						1	A						
900	Z1					5		A	B					
900	Z900-A4													
900	Z900 LTD													

The crude Coyote MB1 with limited performance but better than walking. Built from 1969–71 and sole side valve from big K. Only known photograph is shown here. Are there any left out there?